THE 'I' JUDGMENTS

THE 'I'
JUDGMENTS

Four Sins that Bring About the Fall of Nations
(and the Coming Judgment of America)

Joe Maggelet

NEW VANTAGE
B O O K S

Published by New Vantage Books
An imprint of New Vantage Publishing Partners, Franklin, TN
info@NewVantagePartners.net

Design and typesetting by Webster Creative Group,
Lynnville, TN
Cover photo from iStock

ISBN: 978-0-9909813-1-2
First printing in 2016
Printed in Canada

CONTENTS

ACKNOWLEDGMENTS

Thanks to the many people who have in one way or another contributed to the writing of this book.

Thanks to my friend Dr. Mark Hamilton who, for 25 years, has encouraged me and even tried to convince me that I can write a book. That was laughable to me, really out of my comfort zone, but it has happened. Mark, thanks for the many long conversations and helpful comments! You are a great brother in the Lord.

Thanks to Jesse and Diana Myers who read through the book and "fixed" my many grammar problems. Thanks for being so helpful and prayerful for this endeavor.

Thanks to my friend, Professor Paul Schloemer, who read the manuscript and gave many good suggestions. Thanks for your prayers and help.

Ryan Brown was a constant sounding board for me for two years while thinking and praying about writing this book. Thanks, Ryan, for being so helpful and the many great conversations.

To Renee, my wife, and children, Nathan, Natalie, Nick and Nadia, you have been a great help and support in this endeavor; thanks for loving me and upholding me in prayer.

To the pastors and people of Grace Church in Ashland, Ohio, you don't know how great your support and love have been through this process!

Lastly, thank you to my God and my Lord Jesus for giving me the grace to see this through! *Psalm 90:16–17*

INTRODUCTION

The wicked will return to Sheol, even all the nations that forget God.
—Psalm 9:17

For two weeks of 1979, I sat in a college Old Testament class and listened as the professor daily asked us, "What is so special about Isaiah?" As if in answer to the question he repeated every day, he told us that Isaiah was the greatest of all the prophets—and I believed him. When he came to Isaiah 40:1, in fact, I was so moved by what he explained about the passage that I began to cry. Now, 37 years later, tears still well up in my eyes when I think of how great our God is and what He did in Isaiah 40:1!

So what made Isaiah someone who could be considered "the greatest of all the prophets"? As I see it, God gave him an astounding perspective on the world of his time and the times to come. To reveal the plans God had in mind, He essentially lifted Isaiah up and transported him 150 years into the future, set him down, and said, "Write!" [1] As a result, Isaiah was writing as if he were in the midst of the future Babylonian crisis, and out of his visit to the future, he wrote, "'Comfort, O comfort My people,' says your God" (Isa 40:1). In the prophecy, God had judged His people, Judah, by raising the nation of Babylon to carry Judah into captivity. By sending this message ahead of time through His "advance man" Isaiah, God had a ready-made message for the Jews in exile when the time came. "Comfort, O comfort My people" would become extremely

---

1 Robertson McQuilken, *Understanding and Applying the Bible* (Chicago: Moody Publishers, 2009), 253-272.

relevant to His people in a foreign land.

It was this example of God's judgment of Judah that led to my fascination with the topic of the rise and fall of nations. More specifically, I was fascinated by the God who is big enough to build or destroy whole nations!

The Man at the Top Is Not a Man

Nebuchadnezzar was the Babylonian king God raised up to take Judah into captivity, but He also made sure that Nebuchadnezzar knew who was in charge of the plans. In Daniel 4:17, God revealed His purpose to Nebuchadnezzar: "In order that the living may know that the Most High is ruler over the realm of mankind and bestows it on whomever He wishes and sets over it the lowliest of men" (see also Daniel 4:32, 34-35).

Nebuchadnezzar had to learn an important lesson, a lesson every president, king, ruler, or dictator in all of history should understand: God is in total control of rulers and their nations. No one becomes a leader without God establishing him or her as the head of the nation. Even a nation itself does not exist unless God makes it so. The Ruler above all human rulers is the Lord our God, the God of our fathers Abraham, Isaac, and Jacob.

In that 1979 Old Testament class, I saw clearly for the first time God's perspective on the nations of the world. They are His to use in accord with His plans for humankind. God alone determines the lifespan and purpose of nations. Psalm 22:28 is blunt on this point: "For the kingdom is the Lord's, and He rules over the nations." And Psalm 47:8 says, "God reigns over the nations. God sits on His holy throne."

God has spoken through the prophets to teach nations about their purpose and warn them against presuming to be in charge of their own destinies. Just as Nebuchadnezzar was judged until he learned that God ruled over Babylon, so nations will be disciplined until they learn that God rules over them. Once they accept that lesson, they will be blessed.

As a 19-year-old college student, I was so intrigued by this truth that my thoughts turned to my own country, the United States of America. Were we living out our purpose? Were we being blessed by God because we obeyed that purpose? Were we being judged by God?

Perhaps you remember 1979—or have read about the significant events of the time. Decades into the Cold War, the United States and Soviet Union still threatened one another with nuclear annihilation, and a Middle Eastern country called Iran rocketed onto the front pages in the tumult of selecting a new form of government under a revolutionary leader named Ayatollah Khomeini. He transformed Iran into an anti-American Islamic theocracy. Disdaining the nation that had supported Iran's previous leader, the Shah, Iranians attacked our embassy in Tehran and took 52 Americans hostage. Nearly every night after the November diplomatic outrage, I watched *ABC News* begin each report with anchor Frank Reynolds announcing, "Hostage crisis, day ____." These hostages would not be released until Ronald Reagan became president, more than a year later.

During subsequent years, I became convinced that God was, indeed, judging America, and I wanted to know why. Then I ran across Psalm 9:17: "The wicked will return to Sheol, even all the nations who forget God." There it was in the Psalms—my answer. America was in a process of turning away from the purpose for which the Lord had raised her up.

The realization disturbed me greatly, and my constant prayer for our nation since 1979 has been for repentance. Yet, we still have not returned to the Lord who raised us up in the 1700s, and we have not thanked the Lord our God for all of

His benefits bestowed upon us. Now, in 2016, we have drifted even further than in 1979—and our situation is much more precarious. The difference between 1979 and 2016 is of great importance.

Dual Judgments

God delivers two types of judgments on nations. One I call medicinal judgments and the other, final judgments.

In 1979, the United States was under the medicinal judgments of the Lord. These judgments are intended to open the eyes of a nation's citizenry so they might be healed. Amos 4:7-8 offers an example of a medicinal judgment:

> Furthermore I withheld the rain from you while there were still three months until harvest. Then I would send rain on one city and on another city I would not send rain, one part would be rained on while the other part not rained on would dry up. So two or three cities would stagger to another city to drink water, but you would not be satisfied; yet you would not return to Me declares the Lord.

Medicinal judgments are "bad," but they extend hope to a people.

Fast forward to 2016, though, and we are under a final judgment—a judgment meant to destroy the nation, her government and infrastructure. I have read many books on the subject of the rise and fall of nations, and they are alarming. For example, in *Twilight of a Great Civilization*, Carl F. H. Henry refers to a speech called "The Barbarians Are Coming," which he delivered at Eastern Baptist Theological Seminary in September 1969.[2] In the speech, he talked of the decline of our modern culture and a "swift relapse to paganism." [3] In the areas of science, education, and religion, Henry pointed out that America was going in the wrong direction—and that was in 1969!

Think about what has come to pass since Carl Henry's warning about a relapse into paganism. During the intervening decades, we have witnessed a wholesale turning of our nation towards anti-Christian ethics without considering where these new ethics will take us. And those who warn the nation are attacked and demeaned!

Or consider Francis Schaeffer's *The God Who Is There*. Schaeffer argued that America was suffering from a change in its concept of truth. From the new concept of truth, he explained that "men and women, beginning absolutely by themselves, try rationally to build out from themselves, having only man as their integration point, to find all knowledge, meaning, and value." [4] This new type of thinking excluded absolutes and exalted relativism. Schaeffer predicted that this type of thinking would lead to all forms of immorality becoming accepted as normal in society.

As early as the 1960s, God raised up men to warn America about its dangerous path. Since then, many more have joined the chorus sounding the alarm. In 1994, for example, Jim Nelson Black wrote *When Nations Die* in which he examined the three areas of social decay, cultural decay, and moral decay. Black recounts a conversation that Soviet dissident and world-renowned author Alexander Solzhenitsyn overheard between two peasants in the Soviet Union. "'It is because we have forgotten God. That is why all this is happening to us,'

2 Carl F. H. Henry, *Twilight of a Great Civilization: The Drift Toward Neo-Paganism* (Westchester, IL: Crossway, 1988), copyright page, ix.
3 Ibid., 15.
4 Francis A. Schaeffer, *The God Who Is There* (Downers Grove, IL: IVP, 1968), 9.

5

they said. 'We have forgotten God.'" Solzhenitsyn said he would never forget the wisdom of these simple peasants.[5] As I look at America in 2016, my critique is the same as those two peasants: America has forgotten God, the truth I found in Psalm 9:17.

I am not the only one who has discerned America's "forgetfulness." In 2010, Erwin Lutzer authored *When a Nation Forgets God: Seven Lessons We Must Learn from Nazi Germany.* At the beginning of the book, Lutzer observes:

> I have written this book to show that Nazism did not arise in a vacuum. There were cultural streams that made it possible for this ideology to emerge and gain a wide acceptance by the popular culture. Some of those streams—myths accepted by the masses—are in evidence in America today, and hence this book.[6]

Lutzer points out a key truth—proclaimed in his first chapter title: "When God Is Separated from Government, Judgment Follows."[7]

Since the 1960s, God has been judging America with medicinal judgments meant to heal us and cause us to repent. But we have ignored the message, and since 2004, I believe we have entered the second, more severe, judgment from the Lord.

Final judgments come upon nations in several ways. One is that God removes the power and authority the nation once had. Another way is to remove the nation's power by allowing some other nation to dominate the nation being judged. I will

---

5 Jim Nelson Black, *When Nations Die: Ten Warning Signs of a Culture in Crisis* (Wheaton: Tyndale, 1994), 207.
6 Erwin W. Lutzer, *When a Nation Forgets God: Seven Lessons We Must Learn from Nazi Germany.* (Chicago: Moody Publishers, 2010), 9-10.
7 Ibid., 15.

explore these in more detail later, but I mention it now so you are prepared for the teaching that God is bringing a final judgment on America.

Before I go on, though, you may have a question running through your mind: If so many great books have been written on the subject of warning America, why is this one needed? This book is different than others because my intent is to teach a simple way of understanding how and why God judges a nation. We will focus primarily on a few Bible passages in which God explains His view of nations. God has been gracious to give us a simple outline that I call the four I's:

- Israel

- Idolatry

- Innocents

- Immorality

When a nation crosses a line set by these four "I" words, then she is in grave danger of a final judgment from the Lord. As we explore these, I hope you will be inspired to read the Scriptures, trust in your God, and pray like you have never prayed before!

THE 'I' JUDGMENTS

1

Meet the Four I's

*Do not defile yourselves by any of these things; for by all these the
nations which I am casting out before you have become defiled.*
—Leviticus 18:24

Lest you think I portrayed God's work with nations too
negatively in the Introduction, please understand that in His
sovereignty, He is not just a destroyer of nations. He is also a
nation builder.

His work of creating nations "out of nothing" is best seen
in the Old Testament record of His building Israel. Israel, in
fact, is the baseline for God teaching us about the rise and
fall of nations. The nation of Israel stands in contrast to the
nations of the Egyptians, the Hittites, Girgashites, Amorites,
Caananites, Perizzites, Hivites, and Jebusites, all of whom
were destroyed in God's timing. In several key passages, the
Old Testament reveals how God views nations and how He
moves to destroy them. Most of the teaching spans the
scriptures from Genesis 12 to the book of Joshua. And God
offers a specific summary of His thinking on the subject in
Leviticus 18.

Looking Back to the Future

Four jam-packed verses in the New Testament deliver a
powerful summary of revelation history from Genesis 12 to
Joshua. From Acts 13:16-19, we learn five vital points about
this period.

THE 'I' JUDGMENTS

1. *The God of Israel Chose the Fathers.*

Acts 13:16-17 recounts that "Paul stood up, and motioning with his hand, he said, 'Men of Israel and you who fear God, listen: The God of this people Israel *chose our fathers*'" (emphasis mine). When God chose Abraham, Isaac, and Jacob, He was selecting the forefathers of the nation and made promises to them about the building of the great nation Israel. His promises included provision of the land, growing its national identity, becoming a blessing to other nations, and protection from hostile countries.

2. *God Made Israel Great While in Egypt.*

As Paul's preaching continues in Acts 13:17, we learn that "the God of this people chose our fathers and *made the people great* during their stay in the land of Egypt" (emphasis mine). After Joseph became the number two ruler in Egypt, he eventually brought 70 people to Egypt with him. These 70 people were the beginning of the nation of Israel. During the four centuries they lived in Egypt, the Hebrews grew to more than a million people!

Genesis 15:5 reveals the original promise of God that is fulfilled in this astounding growth of a people group under the adverse conditions of slavery: "And He took him [Abraham] outside and said, 'Now look toward the heavens and count the stars if you are able to count them.' And He said to him, 'So shall your descendants be.'" Moses acknowledges this fulfillment in an address to the Israelites in Deuteronomy 10:22: "Your fathers went down to Egypt seventy persons in all and now the LORD your God has made you as numerous as the stars of heaven."

3. *God Led Israel Out of Egypt, Which He Then Destroyed.*

Paul reflects this part of the story in Acts 13:17 when he says, "The God of this people Israel chose our fathers and made the people great during their stay in the land of Egypt and with an uplifted arm *He led them out from it*" (emphasis mine). Upon delivering the Hebrews, God destroyed Egypt's infrastructure, farms, army, and pride—indeed, their nation. This, too, had been prophesied to Abraham, in Genesis 15:13-14: "God said to Abram, 'Know for certain that your descendants will be strangers in a land that is not theirs, where they will be enslaved and oppressed four hundred years. But I will also judge the nation whom they will serve; and afterward they will come out with many possessions.'" Egypt is the first of eight nations God destroyed.

4. *God Destroyed Seven Nations in the Land of Canaan.*

Acts 13:18-19 reports, "And for a period of about forty years He put up with them in the wilderness. When He had *destroyed seven nations* in the land of Canaan, He distributed their land as an inheritance" (emphasis mine). Israel stayed in the wilderness for 40 years until a generation of people died off. The generation that came out of Egypt had too much of Egyptian beliefs driving their lives. To enter the Promised Land, the Israelites had to become different than the eight nations which God destroyed, so another promise was fulfilled in this fourth point. Genesis 15:15-17 proclaimed, "As for you [Abraham], you shall go to your fathers in peace; you will be buried at a good old age. Then in the fourth generation they will return here, for the iniquity of the Amorite is not yet complete." God makes an important point about Himself and the Amorites. God was patient with the Amorites and would not bring judgment until the time was right. That right and just time to judge the seven nations was when their sin was complete, or fully lived out.

5.   This Took Place Over a Period of 450 Years.

Acts 13:19 draws this portion of the historical review to a close with the assertion: "When He had destroyed seven nations in the land of Canaan, He distributed their land as an inheritance—*all of which took about four hundred and fifty years*" (emphasis mine). During this 450-year span, God reveals the reasons for destroying a nation. The eight nations (Egypt plus the seven in Canaan) were guilty of idolatry, immorality, killing innocents, and oppressing a people in the way Israel had been oppressed by Egypt.

With these points from Genesis 12 to Joshua in mind, Leviticus 18 becomes an especially poignant summary of God's regard for these eight nations. Leviticus 18 catalogues the sins which nations commit that eventually bring His wrath.

Two questions need to be discussed to understand God's view of these sins:

1)   When do these sins bring His wrath?

2)   What makes these sins so grievous that they would bring the wrath of God?

The answers to these questions are of great importance because they reveal both what God has done and what God is doing presently with the nations.

In Leviticus 18:3, God gives us the summary answer to both questions: "You shall not do what is done in the land of Egypt where you lived, nor are you to do what is done in the land of Canaan where I am bringing you; you shall not walk in their statutes." Apparently, whatever the Egyptians were doing led to their judgment by God. And what is it that they were doing? They were committing the four "I" sins. To discover when these sins bring the wrath of God, we will examine each of the four I's in detail.

I #1—Israel

For 400 years, the Israelites lived within Egypt in their own region called the land of Goshen. They ended up there largely because of the Egyptians' disdain for the Israelites' original profession. When Jacob arrived in Egypt, his son Joseph coached him on what to say to the Pharaoh at their first meeting: "You shall say, 'Your servants have been keepers of livestock from our youth even until now, both we and our fathers,' that you may live in the land of Goshen; for *every shepherd is loathsome to the Egyptians*" (Genesis 46:34, emphasis mine). Even though the Israelites moved to their own area apart from the Egyptians, their hosts soon shifted from the attitude of "loathsome" to the action of "oppressing."

Loathsome comes from a Hebrew word which means a disgusting thing or abomination. It is used five times in Levitcus 18. For instance, Leviticus 18:22 says, "You shall not lie with a male as one lies with a female, it is an abomination." And Leviticus 18:26 says, "But as for you, you are to keep My statutes and My judgments, and shall not do any of these abominations, neither the native, nor the alien who sojourns among you." Notice that an attitude like the Egyptians'—hostility toward "the alien"—is specifically condemned by God, and Israel is commanded not to commit the same error. Then in Leviticus 18:27, God makes it clear that He judges those in Canaan for these abominations: "for the men of the land who have been before you have done all these abominations, and the land has become defiled." Leviticus 18:29-30 further warns:

> For whoever does any of these abominations those persons who do so shall be cut off from among their people. Thus you are to keep My charge that you do not practice any of the abominable customs which have been practiced before you so as not to defile yourselves with them, I am the LORD your God.

God makes evident that the ethical customs and statutes of Israel were to be the opposite of Egypt and the seven nations in the Promised Land. God intended that Israel would live in a way antithetical to the Egyptians.

So, the first lesson Israel needed to learn is that a godly nation does not oppress the foreigner in the land. Unfortunately for Israel, other nations have not returned the favor. History is replete with examples of the oppression of Israel in country after country. Although I will address later the specific oppression of Israel by other nations, for now the important takeaway from these verses is that to oppress a people group in a country is a big no-no in God's sight.

I #2—Idolatry

The second thing Egypt did that all of us should reject is to serve false gods. The gods of Egypt were set against the God of Israel, and a battle ensued. That battle ended with the utter destruction of the country of Egypt. Even the way this played out sends a message for those who pay attention. For instance, God sent a plague of frogs on the land. Significantly, the Egyptians worshipped frogs because of the Nile River and the "gods" who controlled the river.[8] Egypt's polytheistic society worshipped many false gods. This sort of practice brings the wrath of God when it becomes the cultural norm and when it is written into law. The laws of Egypt required the people to do things that were simply unacceptable to the Lord.

Look again at the Leviticus 18:3 passage which says, "You are not to walk in their statutes." *Statutes* is a crucial word. It means laws, principles, and cultural practices of the people. So what is the lesson? When violation of the four I's becomes instituted in law, the end of that nation is near. This suggests that grasping the definition of idolatry—as one of the four I's—is critical to discerning God's plan for a nation.

Idolatry is defined in the Ten Commandments, in Exodus 20:3, "You shall have no other gods before Me," and in Exodus 20:4, "You shall not make for yourself an idol." When idolatry is instituted in law, forcing the people of a nation to worship and serve the gods set up by the state, then judgment begins. The time of the Exodus had become the time for God to judge Egypt for the false gods that the Egyptians served.

I #3—Innocents

The seven nations of Canaan also served false gods—mainly Baal and Molech—through an especially heinous practice. Leviticus 18:21 says, "You shall not give any of your offspring to offer them to Molech, nor shall you profane the name of the Lord your God, I am the LORD." This particular form of worshipping false gods alerts us to another sin which God hates: Killing innocent children in the worship of a false god. Now we have third of the "I" words: Killing Innocents.

Killing Innocents can include the murder of innocent

---

8 *The MacArthur Study Bible* (Nashville: Thomas Nelson, 2006), note on Exodus 8:2 specifies, "The frog was the representation, the image, of the goddess Heqt, the wife of the god Khum, the symbol of resurrection and fertility."

people through genocide, abortion, euthanasia, or infanticide. In the days of Moses and Joshua, the worshippers of several false gods killed their babies as a way of worshipping. Today, we worship the false gods of money, convenience, and selfishness by murdering children in the womb. This will bring the wrath of God.

I #4—Immorality

Most of Leviticus 18 is about immorality. God made clear His disgust with the sins of incest, adultery, bestiality, and homosexuality, in large measure because any great nation is built upon strong families that are moral, strong, and faithful. This Leviticus 18 list of sins is especially destructive to the integrity of families, and therefore God is vehemently opposed to them. These sins damage not only the individuals who commit them but also innocent others such as children. Incest obviously cripples the parent-child relationship. Adultery rips apart a husband and wife. Bestiality and homosexuality both repel the very idea of an integrated family.

"Immorality" describes the fundamental nature of relationships in the seven nations which God destroyed. And so it is today. Charles Murray has said, "Illegitimacy is the single most important social problem of our time, and family instability and single parent families are direct contributors to the sociological problems of our day." [9]

So, Israel, Idolatry, Innocents, and Immorality. When these four I's are instituted as law in a nation, then God brings down His wrath.

---

9 Cited in Jim Nelson Black, 28.

A Reasonable Wrath

Now that we have discovered *when* God brings His wrath on a nation, *what* makes these sins so grievous that they would trigger God's final judgment? Leviticus 18:24-25 provides the answer:

Do not defile yourself by any of these things, for by all these the nations which I am casting out before you have become defiled. For the land has become defiled, therefore I have visited its punishment upon it, so the land has spewed out its inhabitants.

The key word in this passage is *defiled*. Defilement is the process by which a person or nation becomes unclean or impure. The word is used 71 times in Leviticus, and the impurity can be sexual, religious, or ceremonial. An example of defilement is given in Genesis 34. A Hivite named Shechem raped Jacob's daughter Dinah, and Genesis 34:5 describes the offense this way: "Now Jacob heard that Shechem had *defiled* Dinah his daughter" (emphasis mine).

Rape defiles people and hurts them deeply. That's why God hates rape. When this and the other behaviors outlined above become acceptable in a country, the land is defiled.

A family, city, or nation can be defiled by the behavior of its people, and this is grievous to God. Why? Proverbs 11:10-11 explains:

When it goes well with the righteous, the city rejoices, and when the wicked perish, there is glad shouting. By the blessing of the upright, a city is exalted, but by the mouth of the wicked it is torn down.

In God's economy, righteousness exalts a nation and righteous people bring a city together to rejoice. Wickedness, however, tears down lives, and it tears down the city. Proverbs 14:34 offers a similar claim: "Righteousness exalts a nation, but sin is a disgrace to any people." Simply put, behavior that defiles a person, city, or nation is a disgrace.

Leviticus 18 describes this sort of despicable behavior with another word that is as bad as defilement. Leviticus 18:30 says, "Thus you are to keep My charge, that you do not practice any of the *abominable* customs which have been practiced before you, so as not to defile yourselves with them; I am the Lord your God" (emphasis mine). God calls these defiling practices *abominable*. A graphic example will explain just what "abominable" means to God.

One day while walking to church, I passed a dead animal on the side of the road. I could smell it before I saw it, and the stench literally made me gag. As I got closer, I had to walk as far on the other side of the road as possible because I actually thought the odor would make me throw up. Abominable sins are like that dead animal. When the people of a land become an abomination, the disgusting smell will cause the land to "spew" them out. God says the stench of the inhabitants' sin is enough to make the land vomit!

Israel was commanded to avoid all of these behaviors because they would lead to destruction, but sadly, Israel got lazy and did not listen. Jeremiah 2:7 says, "I brought you into the fruitful land to eat its fruit and its good things. But you came and defiled My land, and My inheritance you made an abomination." This defilement of the land was because of Idolatry, Immorality, and killing Innocents. Ezekiel 36:17-18 describes a similar situation:

Son of man, when the house of Israel was living in

their own land, they defiled it by their ways and their deeds; their way before Me was like the uncleanness of a woman in her impurity. Therefore, I poured out my wrath on them for the blood which they had shed on the land, because they had defiled it with their idols.

Israel had defiled herself with idolatry by worshipping the Baals. The nation had defiled herself with immorality by committing flagrant harlotry, and she had defiled herself by killing Innocents.

These practices became cultural norms in Israel, but were they the laws? Not exactly. Israel was bound by the laws which God had written down for them in the Torah, but the people repeatedly broke them in grotesque and abominable ways. Their actions demonstrate that even having good laws is not enough for a society bent on pursuing godlessness. The behavior of the people must match the righteousness of their laws to have meaning.

Israel created a culture which defiled the magnificent laws given to her by God. The prophet Hosea speaks directly to this problem in several places. For instance, Hosea 4:1-2 says:

> Listen to the word of the Lord, O sons of Israel, for the Lord has a case against the inhabitants of the land, because there is no faithfulness or kindness or knowledge of God in the land. There is swearing, deception, murder, stealing, and adultery. They employ violence, so that bloodshed follows bloodshed.

The Hebrew people had the Torah, but its laws were not taught or practiced in the land (they had no knowledge of God), so they built a culture that mirrored eight other nations: the Egyptians, Hittites, Girgashites, Amorites, Caananites,

Perizzites, Hivites, and Jebusites.

Now consider Hosea's description in light of American culture today. Swearing, deception, murder, stealing, and adultery are cultural norms in the movies and evident in the news headlines. A quick, mental exercise helps make the point: Compare TV shows of the 1950s with the TV shows of 2016. To say the least, America was cleaner and more wholesome in the 1950s!

The abominable activities of a nation's people affect everything. Hosea 4:3 says, "Therefore the land mourns, and everyone who lives in it languishes along with the beasts of the field and the birds of the sky; and also the fish of the sea disappear." Violating God's standard causes the very ground to "grieve" the people who manage it. What do we see in America today? Is the land mourning? Check the news, and notice the droughts and increase in earthquakes. The ground is grieving.

In summary: God has demonstrated the four I's through what He did with the nation of Israel. Israel has a unique design, position, and law with respect to the rise and fall of nations, and it was Israel to whom God revealed His mandates for all nations. A key figure in this revelation is a prophet through whom God delivered a critical message to all nations. Jeremiah offered a remarkable and pertinent series of prophecies we will explore in the next chapter.

So Far We Have Learned

1. *Definition of the four "I" sins.*

   - *Sin of* Israel: *Oppressing a minority, racism, or treating a people or class of people as less than human.*

   - *Sin of* Idolatry: *Worshipping a god that does not*

exist, who is not the Creator of everything.

- *Sin of killing* Innocents: *Killing people who have not committed a sin worthy of death.*

- *Sin of* Immorality: *Sex outside of marriage (defined as the lifelong union between one man with one woman)—bestiality, fornication, adultery, homosexuality, or incest.*

2. *When these four I's are instituted into law and accepted by a culture, judgment is on the way.*

3. *Defilement is instituting any of the four I's into law, causing disunity, broken relationships, fear, anger, and distrust.*

4. *Abomination is instituting any of the four I's into law that causes the land to "throw up"—natural disasters, famine, drought, etc.*

The 'I' Judgments

2

GOD SPEAKS A WARNING

*At one moment I might speak concerning a nation or
concerning a kingdom to uproot, to pull down, or to destroy it.*
—Jeremiah 18:7

Warnings are as nearly commonplace as eating and sleeping. On my way to the library today, I encountered several stop signs and yellow lights. These are warnings about oncoming traffic that, if not heeded, could result in a deadly crash. Conscientious drivers are thankful for these alerts because they understand the signs and signals are placed along the way for the safety and well-being of travelers.

God has similarly provided warnings to nations heading into danger of His discipline. The warnings are meant to bring repentance and to turn people from the evil of their ways, so that the disaster of a final judgment can be avoided.

Judge by Example

God raised up the nation of Israel and her prophets to teach all nations what God expects from the people of the world. Author Ronald DiProse explains the lessons from Israel this way:

> In the design of God, Israel has a unique position. It was Israel with whom God made His covenant by the call of Abraham. It was Israel to whom God revealed His name and gave His law. It was to Israel that He sent His prophets with their message of judgment

and of grace. [10]

One prophet in particular was raised up to speak to all of the nations: the prophet Jeremiah. God revealed this specific purpose when he first called Jeremiah: "Before I formed you in the womb I knew you, and before you were born I consecrated you; I have appointed you *a prophet to the nations*" (Jeremiah 1:5, emphasis mine).

In the book of Jeremiah, God warns all nations about potential judgment as well as promised blessings, depending on the response of people to His laws. The immediate context of the book is the coming judgment of Judah by the nation of Babylon. At this point in its history, Israel had crossed the line on Idolatry, Immorality, and killing Innocents, and the nation refused to repent. Therefore, a final judgment of God was in order.

I read the book of Jeremiah while in college, particularly studying some of its more famous passages, and although I became fascinated by the book in general, the verses addressing individual nations were especially compelling. These sections affirm that God is in control of the rise and fall of nations—and that nations exist for only as long as God wants them on earth, and no longer. Jeremiah 1:9-10 offers a clear pronouncement to this effect:

> Then the Lord stretched out His hand and touched my mouth, and the Lord said to me, "Behold I have put My words in your mouth. See, I have appointed you this day over the nations and over the kingdoms, to pluck up and to break down, to destroy and to overthrow, to build and to plant."

---

10 Ronald E. Diprose, *Israel and the Church: The Origins and Effects of Replacement Theology.* (Rome: Istitutio Biblico Evangelico Italiano, 2000), 27.

He also demonstrates this in action among specific nations. Jeremiah 25:1, for instance, speaks of "the word that came to Jeremiah concerning all the people of Judah, in the fourth year of Jehoiakim the son of Josiah, king of Judah (that was the first year of Nebuchadnezzar king of Babylon)." This passage mentions two kings of two different nations whose reigns overlap each other. In his first year as king, Nebuchadnezzar attacked Jehoiakim and took him captive. We find God's commentary on this in Daniel 1:2:

> And the Lord gave Jehoiakim king of Judah into his [Nebuchadnezzar's] hand, along with some of the vessels of the house of God; and he brought them to the land of Shinar, to the house of his god, and he brought the vessels into the treasury of his god.

This conflict between Nebuchadnezzar and Jehoiakim was determined by the power of the Lord, the God of Israel—it was He who gave Jehoiakim into the hand of Nebuchadnezzar.

Submitting to the Inevitable

God's rule over the nations in that area of the world is described in Jeremiah 27:1-7. It teaches us the principle that the God of Israel is in charge of all nations—whether they recognize it or not! It's a fascinating read:

> In the beginning of the reign of Zedekiah the son of Josiah, king of Judah, this word came to Jeremiah from the Lord, saying—thus says the Lord to me— "Make for yourself bonds and yokes and put them on your neck, and send word to the king of Edom, to

the king of Moab, to the king of the sons of Ammon, to the king of Tyre, and to the king of Sidon by the messengers who come to Jerusalem to Zedekiah king of Judah. And command them to go to their masters, saying, 'Thus says the Lord of hosts, the God of Israel, thus you shall say to your masters, "I have made the earth, the men and the beasts which are on the face of the earth by My great power and by My outstretched arm, and I will give it to the one who is pleasing in My sight. And now I have given all these lands into the hand of Nebuchadnezzar king of Babylon, My servant, and I have given him also the wild animals of the field to serve him. And all the nations shall serve him and his son, and his grandson, until the time of his own land comes; then many nations and great kings will make him their servant."'"

This passage lists six nations which were instructed by the Lord to submit to Babylon because God had made her the dominant power for a specific timeframe. Once that time had passed, another nation would rise to rule. God's counsel to these nations is that if they submitted to Babylon, Babylon's rule over them would be peaceful, but if they rebelled, they would surely be destroyed.

God, the creator of nations, rules over the affairs of men. When He speaks, the best thing for hearers to do is to humble themselves and bow to whichever kingdom the Lord has raised up. This requires that nations recognize the need to submit to a dominant nation. Otherwise, disaster will be the inevitable result.

Not Just for Israel

We see through Jeremiah that God speaks to all nations, but now let's turn our attention specifically to how Israel fits into the picture. God raised up Israel as the messenger to all of the Gentile nations. He had promised that in Abraham the Gentiles would be blessed, and He blessed them with information regarding how any nation could be successful. And the takeaway? Heed the lesson and be blessed; reject it and your nation will be cursed!

Consider these passages that reveal the importance of Israel to the Gentile nations:

- Deuteronomy 32:8—"When the Most High gave the nations their inheritance, when He separated the sons of man, He set the boundaries of the peoples according to the number of the sons of Israel."

- Numbers 23:9b—"Behold, a people who dwells apart, and will not be reckoned among the nations." (God has set apart Israel for the good of all the Gentile nations. This setting apart is for the blessing of Israel and for all the nations.)

- Psalm 66:7—"He rules by His might forever; His eyes keep watch on the nations; Let not the rebellious exalt themselves."

This is a direct word to the Gentile nations: Humble yourself under the mighty hand of God. God used the Jewish prophets to teach, train, and warn all Gentile nations about their purpose and place in the world.

There is an inherent warning in God's presentation of

these principles: If you allow anti-Semitism to keep you from learning these lessons, then all of the curses of the Bible will come upon you. Similarly, if you are a Christian and wrongly assume this Old Testament teaching has nothing to do with you or your nation, then you are rebelling against the God who saved you. God has spoken and is speaking to the nations even now. The only appropriate response is humility and repentance.

According to Jeremiah 18:1-10, God continues to speak to nations. The passage can be broken down into two sections: One in which God is speaking to Israel (vv. 1-6) and one in which God is speaking to the rest of the nations (vv. 7-10). We'll look at each section in turn.

God was fond of using word pictures with Jeremiah to show exactly what He was up to. In the first demonstration, God told Jeremiah to visit a potter. When Jeremiah arrived at the potter's house, the artisan was making a vessel on a pottery wheel. The potter then remade the vessel because it was ruined. This picture revealed that God can do whatever He wants with His people Israel, just like a potter can do whatever he wants with his clay. This is also taught plainly in Jeremiah 18:5-6, which says:

> Then the word of the Lord came to me saying, "Can I not, O house of Israel, deal with you as this potter does?" declares the Lord. "Behold, like the clay in the potter's hand, so are you in My hand, O house of Israel."

But this lesson extends beyond the people of Israel. Psalm 47:8 says, "God reigns over the nations, God sits on His holy throne." Israel had to learn that God ruled over them, and the Gentile nations needed to learn exactly the same lesson.

While the outline of Jeremiah 18:7-10 is fairly simple,

it is also profound for the life of any nation. First, God emphasizes the fact that He does speak to people (vv. 7,9). His communication comes in the context of two opposite plans. In the first context, God speaks about "uprooting, pulling down, or destroying a nation or kingdom" (v. 7). Notice that God focuses on the destruction of a nation. If the nation listens and repents, then the destruction will not come, but if it does not repent, destruction is inevitable.

The whole book of Jonah is an example of this type of message. Jonah was sent to the nation of Assyria and her capital city, Nineveh, and his message was remarkably straightforward: "Yet forty days and Nineveh will be overthrown" (Jonah 3:4). It had the desired effect, and the people of Nineveh, from the king down to the slave, repented and turned to God. The story is an example of God acting according to the principle revealed in Jeremiah 18:8: "If that nation against which I have spoken turns from its evil, I will relent concerning the calamity I planned to bring on it." Nineveh turned from its evil, and God relented.

But Jonah was not the only prophet to address Nineveh. Nahum also spoke to Nineveh, and he promised destruction to the nation. Nahum recounts that, after hearing Jonah and experiencing the grace of God, Nineveh turned back to her former sins: Idolatry, Immorality, and killing Innocents. As a result, Nahum issues this warning:

> The Lord has issued a command concerning you: "Your name will no longer be perpetuated. I will cut off idol and image from the house of your gods. I will prepare your grave, for you are contemptible." (Nahum 1:14)

Here God says He will destroy them for their Idolatry, but

God then mentions Immorality and killing Innocents as well, in 3:1,4: "Woe to the bloody city, completely full of lies and pillage; . . . All because of the many harlotries of the harlot." Notice that after an unspecified time, God sent the prophet to tell them they were going to receive a final judgment from the Lord.

What do we learn from this pattern? A nation can repent of the Idolatry, Immorality, and killing of Innocents and be confident that God will keep His promise to withhold His wrath. But if that same nation later fools itself by thinking it can go back to the sinful behavior, judgment is back on the table. In this case, Jeremiah 18:10 came true for Nineveh: "If it does evil in My sight by not obeying My voice, I will think better of the good with which I had promised to bless it."

Today, the city of Nineveh is known as Mosul. During the summer of 2014, Mosul was taken over again by a foreign power named ISIS (Islamic State of Iraq and Syria) which, at the time of this writing, is still fighting a civil war in Iraq. Psalm 9:6 describes the uprooting and destruction of Nineveh: "The enemy has come to an end in the perpetual ruins, and Thou hast uprooted the cities; The very memory of them has perished."

These days, does anybody talk about the city of Nineveh or her great kings? Hardly. When is the last time you saw people clamoring to go to Mosul? No—only if they have a death wish. Nineveh is used today in history classes and Bible studies only as an example of a nation God spoke to in preparation for its destruction.

A similar example is shown in 1 Kings 11 with Jeroboam the son of Nebat. In judging Solomon for his sins, God raised up Jeroboam, as explained in verse 31:

And he said to Jeroboam, "Take for yourself ten pieces;

> for thus says the LORD, the God of Israel, 'Behold, I
> will tear the kingdom out of the hand of Solomon and
> give you ten tribes.'"

This marks the time at which Israel was divided into two nations, Israel and Judah. In 1 Kings 11:38, God says to Jeroboam:

> Then it will be that if you listen to all that I command
> you and walk in My ways, and do what is right in My
> sight by observing My statutes and My command-
> ments, as My servant David did, then I will be with
> you and build you an enduring house as I built for
> David, and I will give Israel to you.

Unfortunately, Jeroboam did not listen to the Lord, and he rebelled. As a result, the blessing of a restored kingdom never came. Instead, God fulfilled what He said in Jeremiah 18. In fact, this pattern repeated itself over and over. There were no faithful kings in Israel. All of them rebelled against the Lord until her destruction by the Assyrians.

Close to Home

In addition to delivering specific messages through His prophets, God also unveils His purposes through His providential work in history. Let's use the Exodus as an example.

When a Pharaoh arose that did not know Joseph, Egypt failed as a nation. It failed because Egypt did not remember all the good God had done for the nation through Joseph, God's representative. The Egyptians forgot that, although the nation faced seven years of drought, God had blessed them through Joseph's leadership. And when Egypt set aside that part of her history, trouble was on the way.

Likewise, America faces a huge crisis in disregarding the providential work of God. Our history books have all but eliminated the Lord's handiwork in raising up leaders to create the United States of America. As our children are increasingly taught views of history that eliminate God, idolatry is at the forefront of American education.

We would do well to listen and learn from the young man who spoke to a mob in New York on the evening of April 4, 1865 after President Lincoln was shot. Distraught at what had happened to the president, people listened carefully as a man stood up to address them:

> Fellow Citizens! Clouds and darkness are round about Him! His pavilion are dark waters and thick clouds of the skies! Justice and Judgment are the habitation of His throne! Mercy and truth shall go before His face. Fellow Citizens! God reigns and the government of Washington still lives![11]

Future president James A. Garfield was the young man who directed the thoughts of these Americans to the Lord at a time of great disaster.

For most of our history, public schools taught the providential work of God. History books included quotes like this one from founding father James Madison:

> The belief in a God all powerful, wise, and good, is so essential to the moral order of the world and to the happiness of man that arguments which enforce it cannot be drawn from too many sources nor adapted

11 Robert Granville Caldwell, *James A. Garfield: Party Chieftan* (New York: Dodd and Mead Company, 1965), 155-156.

with too much solicitude to the different characters and capacities impressed with it. . . . We have staked the whole future of American civilization not upon the power of government, far from it. We have staked the future upon the capacity of each and all of us to govern ourselves, to sustain ourselves according to the Ten Commandments of God.[12]

Benjamin Franklin offered a similar assessment: "If men are so wicked as we now see them with religion what would they be without it? Only a virtuous people are capable of freedom."[13]

Abraham Baldwin, a signer of the Constitution of the United States, a member of Congress, a U.S. Senator, statesman, lawyer, and educator likewise said:

When the minds of the people in general are viciously disposed and unprincipled and their conduct disorderly, a free government will be attended with greater confusions and evils more horrid than the wild, uncultivated state of nature. It can only be happy when the public principles and opinions are properly directed and their manners regulated. This is an influence beyond the reach of laws and punishments and can be claimed only by religion and education. It should therefore be among the first objects of those who wish well to the national prosperity to encourage and support the principles of religion and morality and early to place the youth under the forming hand of society, that by instruction they may be molded to

---

12 Cited in Os Guiness, *The American Hour: A Time of Reckoning and the Once and Future Role of Faith* (New York: Free Press, 1993), 151.
13 Ibid., 144.

the love of virtue and good order."[14]

Since God has essentially been eradicated from the public schools of America, can it be long before we become the wild and uncultivated people predicted by Baldwin? America has left the God of her founding and has denied His voice these last 55 years. Yet God is still speaking to the nations through His Word and through His providential work in history. God is telling America about the four I's. The question is: Are we listening?

What We Have Learned So Far

1. *God speaks to all nations.*

2. *God raises up nations and brings nations down.*

3. *God expects nations to accept His sovereignty regarding which nations He raises up and which ones He puts down.*

4. *God expects all nations to accept that Israel is the messenger nation, teaching all nations about proper behavior.*

5. *God expects the nations to repent when He speaks to them.*

14 William J. Federer, *America's God and Country* (Muscle Shoals, AL: Fame Publishing, Inc., 1994), 33-34.

3

GOD PREACHES JUDGMENT

*The wicked will return to Sheol even
all the nations who forget God.*—Psalm 9:17

In the last chapter, we saw that before the Lord brings judgment on a nation, He speaks to that nation. So the question arises: If America is in danger and God is speaking to us, what is He saying? To explore the answer, we will look to the prophet Amos.

A prophet to Israel's southern kingdom of Judah, Amos's assignment was a tough one: To go up north to his brothers and deliver a message of judgment. The way God delivered the message is especially pertinent for our purpose of learning how God speaks to nations, because from it, we learn both how God speaks and what He says to people in danger of judgment.

The Judgment Equation

Through Amos, God spoke to eight nations, using this formula: "Thus says the Lord, for three transgressions of Damascus and for four I will not revoke its punishment" (Amos 1:3). This blueprint for judgment follows the same pattern as the message given in Genesis 15:16 regarding the Amorites: "Then in the fourth generation they will return here, for the iniquity of the Amorite is not yet complete." Restating this in Amos's terms: The three sins of the Amorites had built up their iniquity; the fourth sin caused the iniquity to be complete. This pattern, also referenced by other prophets as a cup being filled, applies to each nation in Amos's prophecy as it fills up its measure of sin. When the sin cup gets to the point of overflowing, God's judgment arrives.

Though God addresses all eight nations with the same formula, each one hears a unique reason for its punishment. Each nation "specialized" in a particular version of judgment-worthy wrongdoing. The first six nations addressed by Amos were those surrounding Israel and Judah. Their offenses were:

- *Damascus* threshed Gilead with implements of sharp iron;

- *Gaza* deported an entire population to Edom;

- *Tyre* delivered up an entire population to Edom; they neglected the covenant of brotherhood;

- *Edom* pursued his brother with the sword and stifled his compassion;

- *Ammon* ripped open the pregnant women of Gilead;

- *Moab* burned the bones of the king of Edom to lime.

In each case, God confronts them on various acts of murder, immorality, and idolatry. God mentions their false gods in several places as well as their wicked motivations, and despite the variety of sins committed, the common thread is that all are being judged based on the law written on their consciences.

God judges the nations who do not have the Word of God differently than those who do. Romans 1 and 2 make this distinction when it says:

- "because that which is known about God is evident within them; for God made it evident to them" (1:19).

- "For when Gentiles who do not have the Law do instinctively the things of the Law, these not having the Law, are a law to themselves, in that they show the work of the Law written in their hearts, their conscience bearing witness and their thoughts alternately accusing or else defending them" (2:14-15).

The first six nations are judged on behavior that they intuitively know is wrong. They had to ignore their consciences and close their hearts to conduct themselves the way they did. Yes, they all worshipped false gods, but that alone does not bring a final judgment. If worshipping a false god brought the wrath of God immediately, God would not have waited 450 years to judge the seven nations in Canaan!

So what is it that fills a nation's cup of sin to overflowing? It is when the worship of false gods leads to such hatred and anger that the nation begins to kill whole populations. Stifling all human dignity and mercy, these people crossed the line into despicable behavior. When a whole people group gets to the point that they murder, pillage, and kill to defend their "gods," a final judgment is on the horizon.

By contrast with these six nations, Israel and Judah are judged by a different standard. Notice the contrast:

- *Judah* rejected the law of the Lord;

- *Israel* sold the righteous for money and profaned "My Holy Name."

The first six nations are judged on the basis of fundamental human compassion, while the last two are judged because of specific revelation. To the first six nations, God says, "Stop treating each other in such cruel and wicked ways." But to

Judah and Israel, He says, "Be faithful to the revelation which you received from God."

The judgment of God led to the destruction of each of these nations. In each case, God said He was going to send fire upon their house. "House" here means the line of kings that was currently ruling in each of these nations, and it means the capital cities—often mentioned by name—which were the seats of power.

Something Feels Wrong about This

How does God speak to the first six nations? Their consciences bear witness, and people have a gnawing feeling that something is wrong. God begins by sending lesser judgments on the people to wake them up. These judgments can come in the form of national disasters, financial distress, war, or cultural breakdowns. For the most part, they are passive judgments.

A passive judgment of the Lord is like someone putting water in the gas tank of a new car. You might say to yourself, "I will do this my way, and my way is to drive the car with water in the gas tank." This sort of rebellious attitude is ridiculous, but it is how God's passive judgment works. He turns people over to the hardness of their hearts, and they fail miserably at life. In some situations, the natural consequences of sin are sufficient judgment.

Romans 1:24 describes such a judgment: "Therefore God gave them over in the lusts of their hearts to impurity, that their bodies might be dishonored among them." And in verse 26: "For this reason God gave them over to degrading passions." Although we call it a passive judgment, notice that it is actually God doing something. He is giving people what they want.

When passive judgment occurs, an active evil presence

will begin to emerge. The story of Job depicts how the process of passive judgment develops. Job was a righteous man who was attacked by Satan when God gave the devil permission to do so. Previously, God had been protecting Job by putting a hedge around his possessions and his body. First, God removed the protective hedge around Job's possessions and family, and Satan attacked his servants, children, and livestock. Next, God removed the hedge from Job's health, and Satan attacked Job's body. Although Job was not being judged for any sin he committed, this shows the same progression of suffering that can come with passive judgments. Job, of course, was persevering for a bigger prize. His heart was right with God, and the suffering led to greater trust and love for God.

A person or nation facing the passive judgment of God because of rebellion and dedication to evil will not only face suffering from the natural consequences of sin, but also will face the evil and hatred of Satan and his minions. When God turns people over to the lusts of their own hearts, they experience great dishonor. This is how it works out with each of the major categories of judgment:

1—Idolatry

- The false god never lives up to your expectations.
- The false god expects too much of you.
- The false god fails you again and again.

2—Immorality

- Lust and sins of the flesh increase.
- Dissatisfaction with sex and lust will become

pronounced.

- Dissatisfaction leads to a quest for more gratification.

- Lewdness, perverseness, drunkenness, drug abuse, and a life out of control are the hallmarks of this passive judgment.

3—Killing Innocents

- Anger and hatred begins to grow.

- Desire to shut up those who oppose your anger, hatred, and toleration of murder increases.

- More killing is the result.

4—Israel

- Racism causes more racism.

- Racism turns to violence.

- Violence turns to murder and a holocaust.

This is where Satan will take any person or nation who is under the passive judgment of God.

The satanic pattern develops in Egypt in Exodus 1. Satan knows from the prophecy to Abraham that it is time for God to take Israel out of Egypt and bring the people to the Promised Land. (Satan can count to 400, so he has been counting the years.) Since his goal is to stop the work of God, what does he do?

First, Satan inspires Pharaoh to wipe out the baby boys to prevent God (so Satan thinks) from raising up a leader. Pharaoh was a willing participant. In his hard-heartedness, he ignored history and "knew not Joseph." Since he was willing to forget what God had done through Joseph and since Pharaoh set himself up as a god, God hardened his heart and turned him over to the devil. Like their leader, the Egyptians became hard-hearted and hated the Jews, enslaving and oppressing them. Two Egyptian women, however, were not so hardened: the midwives Shiprah and Puah. Pharaoh told them to put the baby Hebrew boys to death but to let the girls live. Shiprah and Puah, however, did not obey Pharaoh because they feared God. They let the boys live, and Exodus 1:20-21 tells God's response: "So God was good to the midwives, and the people multiplied, and became very mighty. And it came about because the midwives feared God, that He established households for them."

The lesson is clear to all who will pay attention. The people of a nation under the discipline and wrath of God need to learn from the two midwives: No matter what your leaders command, you should fear God and do what is right.

As I mentioned, though, Israel and Judah were under a totally different set of rules. Like Judah and Israel, any nation which has the Word of God is under greater responsibility and subject to greater judgment. America is one such country.

No Exceptions to the Rule

America is under the discipline of God because she has the Word of God. Like Russia in 1917 and Germany in 1940, America faces pressure from the Lord God because we refuse to repent and turn to Him. Before the Bolshevik Revolution, Russia had a thousand-year-long Christian heritage, and yet she rejected the Word of the Lord. The Russian people perverted the Word of God, oppressed and murdered the Jews, and would not heed the call of God to turn and repent. This led to 70 years of rule under atheistic communism.

Likewise, Germany rejected the Word and chose to follow the state as a nationalistic idol. Christians who stood against that perverted philosophy were in the minority before World War I and World War II. They warned the nation, pleading with Germany to turn from her idolatry and the killing of innocents, but to no avail. Germany, who inherited a legacy of great witnesses to the truth of God and great preachers and teachers, perverted the Word and rejected the law of God. Then, utter destruction came upon the nation. The "thousand-year" Reich lasted 12 years, and in those 12 years, the state grew more and more contemptible until the whole nation was put down like a hunter puts down a rabid dog.

God judged Russia by giving her an atheistic government that matched her sinful desires, and He judged Germany by total destruction at the hands of the combined Allied powers. God uses a variety of ways to bring final judgment upon a nation.

America is at a time in her history that she is facing the wrath of the Lord, and there's no biblical reason to think we will be the one country in history that has not been judged according to God's righteousness. Many books have been written over the last 50 years describing the crisis we are experiencing, yet every year it gets worse and our crisis more intense. And what, exactly, is this crisis?

Os Guiness, in his excellent book *The American Hour* says, "A generation that fails to read the signs of the times may be forced to read the writing on the wall."[15] Guiness describes the problem facing America as a "crisis of cultural authority," saying, "Just say 'no' is America's most urgently needed slogan at the very moment in her history when, 'Why Not?' is

---

15 Guiness, 414.

America's most unanswerable question."[16] Guiness explains the crisis this way:

> [U]nder the impact of modernity, the beliefs, ideals, and traditions that have been central to Americans and to American democracy—whether religious, such as Jewish and Christian beliefs, or civic, such as Americanism—are losing their compelling cultural power. This crisis is not a crisis of legitimacy, like that of the Soviet Union, but a crisis of vitality that goes to the heart of America's character and strength.[17]

I believe that, much like Babylon in the days of Nebuchadnezzar when God said the nation would fall under the rule of his grandson, we are in our last days as the dominant world power. It has come not just because we have denied the faith of our forefathers, nor has it come simply because we have let opportunities slip through our hands. It has come because we have rebelled against the living God.

Refusing to Take Our Medicine

God has been faithful to the American people. He sent medicinal judgments our way, so we would wake up, but we have rebelled again and again. We are surely like what 1 Timothy 4:1 describes: "But the Spirit explicitly says that in later times some will fall away from the faith paying attention to deceitful spirits and doctrines of demons." The medicinal judgments have been in place from 1960 to 2004 and mirror what the Lord did in Amos 4.

In the fourth chapter of Amos, God catalogues a series of

---

16 Ibid., 27, 29.
17 Ibid., 27.

medicinal judgments, each of which is followed by the refrain, "Yet you have not returned to Me, declares the Lord." God describes five instances when He sent a problem to the nation, and the nation's response was to rebel against the Lord. In each case, the Lord wanted his firstborn son, Israel, to return and be healed. The medicinal judgments included drought, small wars, assassinations, and plagues. After four of the last seven kings of Israel were assassinated, God finally gave this admonition to Israel, in Amos 4:12: "Prepare to meet your God!" Soon afterward, Israel was taken into captivity at the hand of the Assyrians.

To bring these principles into modern times and to see how they are playing out in America, I start the chronology in the 1960s because that is when the four "I" sins ramped up in our culture. During the 1960s, the sins of Idolatry, Immortality, killing Innocents, and the hatred of Israel began. I mention Israel because of the conflict it entered during that period, and the conflict has not yet ended. The battle for Jerusalem began in 1967, and it will continue until Jesus comes back.

Immorality also increased in the 1960s as the pill, adultery, and fornication began to be promoted as normal, natural, and "morally acceptable" like never before. This era of growing promiscuity ushered in the desire to abort children, so not long after the "sexual revolution," Americans were granted the legal right to kill babies.

Likewise, Idolatry came to the forefront in the 1960s when America sought to divorce herself from the God of the Bible. In the midst of these trends, God began sending medicinal judgments.

You'll recall that the intent of medicinal judgments is to heal a nation. The cataloging of our sins should cause us to look to Him. Since God is the Creator of all things and since He rules over all events, both good and evil, we should see these happenings as coming from the sovereign hand of God. The comparison to the list in Amos is hard to ignore.

In 1963, President Kennedy was shot and killed in Dallas, Texas. Remember that the reason for judgment on Nebuchadnezzar personally was "in order that the living may know that the Most High is ruler over the realm of mankind, and bestows it on whom He wishes, and sets over it the lowliest of men" (Daniel 4:17b). God called for the removal of John F. Kennedy as our president, and the nation mourned for him. I was three years old at the time, and his death is one of my earliest memories. I recall seeing my mother cry, and people everywhere seemed to be talking about it.

The Kennedy assassination is an important event in our history because God will treat the nation in the way a leader rules over the people. If the ruler rules with righteousness, then God will bless the nation. Even if the nation does not follow after the leader, God will still bless the nation that has a righteous ruler. On the other hand, if the ruler is unrighteous, then the nation is in trouble.

John F. Kennedy was unrighteous in many ways. He was an adulterer,[18] and although this cheating on his wife was protected by the press and those closest to him, his actions reflected what many Americans were doing in private. Adultery and fornication were on the increase in America.

Larry Kelley, author of *Lessons from Fallen Civilizations*, says there are ten immutable laws which govern civilizations. The first is that "No nation has ever survived once its citizenry ceased to believe its culture worth saving."[19] In that light, perhaps it is fitting that President Kennedy was assassinated by Lee Harvey Oswald, a lover of the Soviet Union, progres-

18 Mimi Alford, *Once upon a Secret: My Affair with President John F. Kennedy and Its Aftermath*. (New York: Random House, 2013).

19 Larry Kelley, *Lessons from Fallen Civilizations: Can a Bankrupt America Survive the Current Islamic Threat?* (Englewood, CO: Hugo House, 2012), 25.

sive thought, and the belief system which holds that the state should regulate every aspect of the private sector.[20]

The 1950s saw the development of a dividing line between two groups of people. On one side was William F. Buckley who claimed that the progressives and "the Yale faculty were overwhelmingly hostile to Judeo-Christendom and capitalism and something should be done about it."[21] On the other side was Arthur Schlesinger, Jr., who wrote *This Vital Center* and advocated for the progressives.[22] Unfortunately for President Kennedy, he was in the progressive party (Democrats) but espoused anti-communist doctrines. The result was his assassination at the hand of Lee Harvey Oswald, a committed communist.

I believe the social unraveling that started in the 1950s, will eventually lead to the destruction of America. Why? The United States had a decision to make on November 23, 1963 (the day after President Kennedy was assassinated) which would forever determine her future—the decision between accepting atheistic communism and reviving a Judeo-Christian republic. Since then, we have continued to draw closer to communism and have slowly dismantled our Judeo-Christian republic. Commenting on this shift, Jim Black says:

> [T]he deterioration of moral, economic, and religious vitality in contemporary culture has been a slow and withering process. It would be hard to pinpoint a precise starting point, but the 1920's is a good rough estimate. The real atrophy, however, began in the 1960's and has been gathering momentum for the

---

20 Ibid., 184.
21 Ibid., 185.
22 Arthur Schlesinger, Jr, *The Vital Center: The Politics of Freedom* (Boston: Houghton Mifflin, 1962).

past thirty years.[23]

Since Black wrote *When Nations Die* in 1994, we have "crossed the Rubicon" and are standing in the floodplain, ready to be washed away.

Since JFK's death, many progressives have claimed that the president was killed by the radical right because progressives did not want to admit the truth—that Kennedy was killed by one of their own. The progressives have "progressed" from irrationality to a total loss of civic virtue. That is not to say that President Kennedy was a model of rationality. After all, he advocated Christian ethics while betraying his wife and, arguably by doing so, his own country. His administration heralded "a giant leap for mankind" toward the disintegration of virtue in America.

At Kennedy's death, Lyndon B. Johnson took over the presidency and advanced the cause of progressive atheism while betraying our deepest held beliefs and traditions as Americans. He involved us in the Vietnam War, which became a disaster for United States. All the while, the Soviet Union actively opposed the U.S. by conducting a misinformation campaign all over the world. Sympathetic to the progressive cause, the press naively or unwittingly repeated the lies. Division and lack of unity undermined American effectiveness during the Vietnam War, and the trend haunts us to this day.

As anti-American riots hit the streets during the Vietnam War, we had a chance to repent in response to the preaching of Francis Schaeffer, Billy Graham, Martin Lloyd Jones, Carl F. H. Henry, and other biblically-sound men of God, but we refused. Then, God raised up another national leader named Richard Nixon whose Watergate scandal brought America to

---

23 Jim Black, *When Nations Die: Ten Warning Signs of a Culture in Crisis* (Wheaton: Tyndale, 1994), 208-209.

a new low. The nation was not only divided, but loss of confidence in the government seemed to grow, by the hour. We lost one president by assassination and another through resigning in disgrace. Ungodly leaders could not seem to make up their minds whether to take us toward progressive atheism or Judeo-Christian culture.

As these tragedies unfolded, God was raising up His representatives who called America to repent. Not long after I started college in 1977, I heard this statement, attributed to Ruth Graham: "If God does not judge America, He will have to apologize to Sodom and Gomorrah." Whether she or someone else said it, the statement was symptomatic of the day, and if it was at all true in 1977, it is absolutely true today!

The next medicinal judgment sent upon America by God is truly frightening because it still haunts us. Jimmy Carter is the perfect example of a man who succumbed to the deceptions of progressive atheism all the while claiming to esteem Judeo-Christian values. He stood up to Soviet expansionism like a snowball in Florida. To say he is the weakest president in our history would be an understatement. Under his watch, America faced many crises, but none graver than what happened in Iran in 1979. When Iranian revolutionaries attacked our embassy in Tehran and kidnapped our citizens, Jimmy Carter did nothing. That a president would not act in the face of such hostility is especially sobering in light of the truth I mentioned earlier that "no nation has ever survived once its citizenry ceased to believe its culture worth saving."[24]

President Carter had acted against his own country when he attacked and emasculated the CIA with the Church Committee hearings and the Rockefeller Commission. Kelley outlines the destruction foisted on our ability to defend ourselves through intelligence gathering:

---

24 Kelley, 184.

At the time a third of the agency resigned, Carter hindered the nation from protecting itself. He stated that he was at war with his own intelligence service. Six hundred positions in covert espionage were shut down. In 1978, Congress passed the Foreign Intelligence Surveillance Act (FISA) that required a court order for electronic monitoring of foreign nationals, even those located in the USA.[25]

What a win for our enemies! President Carter did not believe our culture worth saving and was all too willing to appease enemies like Iran. Immutable Law #3 in Larry Kelley's *Lessons from a Fallen Civilization* states that, "Appeasement of a ruthless outside power always invites aggression. Treaties made with ruthless despots are always fruitless and dangerous."[26] President Carter appeased the Ayatollah Khomeni, even preferring him to the Shah, the previous leader of Iran. As Kelley observes:

> During the 1970s, while the Shah was a close American ally in the Cold War, Ayatollah Khomeini operated out of France. He distributed vast numbers of sermons to mosques and receptive congregations in Iran and other Shiite enclaves throughout the Islamic world. As a result, it was common knowledge throughout the Middle East that Khomeini had a five step plan to conquer the West and destroy the Great Satan (the USA). Andrew Young, Carter's ambassador to the U.N. called Khomeini a saint.[27]

25 Ibid., 131.
26 Ibid.
27 Ibid., 267.

The appeasement of the Ayatollah Khomeini has led to untold disaster for America. Each year, Iran holds a conference called "Death to America, Death to Israel." As Americans were held hostage in Iran—mistreated and abused by a brutal dictatorship—so today America is held hostage by our refusal to repent. As a result, there are now two major enemies and two rival faiths seriously dividing America: Progressive Atheism and Jihadist Islam.

To bring the Iran disaster fully into the present, President Barack Obama signed a deal with Iran that furthers its plan to destroy America. Negotiated with the six nations known as P5+1 (France, the United Kingdom, United States, Russia, and China, plus Germany), this deal gives Iran several advantages for her goals to destroy America and Israel. First, it advances the relationship between Iran and Russia. After the deal was signed, Russia agreed to send Iran her S-300 missile defense system, an advanced system intended to stop Israel or America from attacking Iranian nuclear facilities. Second, it strengthens the enemies of Israel. As Iran stands to gain $150 billion from the arrangement, some of that money will doubtless find its way to Hezbollah, Hamas, and anyone else who is willing to destroy the Jewish people and their country. Third, the deal does not even seek to stop the terrorism which the Iranian regime so blatantly professed as her right during the negotiations. Iran went so far as to say her desire to destroy Israel was not negotiable. Fourth, despite public realtions spin to the contrary, the deal does not ensure inspections. Although press reports say the inspections could be held anytime and anywhere, side deals were made to guarantee that Iran can do its own "inspections." Finally, there are no sanctions specified, even if Iran violates the terms of the agreement. I read much of the agreement, and I am appalled that America would agree to such a feckless and weak arrangement. I told my wife and others that the agreement can lead to only one thing: war.

No Turning Back

If ever we needed a national revival, it was in 1979. The disaster brewing for America was heating up then, but America's pride in her power and riches had blinded her to the danger lurking in our land. When God is ready to send a final judgment to a nation, he advances its enemies and gives them open doors to attack. In 2015, the enemies of America were greatly strengthened, and they are ready to attack the homeland.

The recent personal history of one man offers a small-scale parallel to what God would want the outcome to be for a nation facing medicinal judgments. A key participant in the Nixon Watergate scandal, Chuck Colson went to jail for his crimes, and while in prison, he became a Christian. Colson had been a man driven to protect the President, find dirt on political enemies, and destroy those whom he deemed to be the President's rivals. He was committed to political solutions employing ethics and morals from the dark side, but Colson lost his power, prestige, freedom, and the identity he had created for himself when officials marched him off to jail. Through Colson's prison conversion experience, God raised up this man to be a witness to the nation. In 1976, he wrote a book called *Born Again* to tell of his changed life.[28] The message to America should have been clear: You will not solve your problems by unethical, evil, wicked pursuit of power, but you will solve it by repenting and turning to the faith of your fathers.

Colson started a ministry to inmates called Prison Fellowship, and the organization has flourished over the last 35 years,

---

28 Charles W. Colson, *Born Again*. (Lincoln, VA: Chosen Books, 1978).

but during those same years, the United States has languished
and faltered. We have had chance after chance to repent as a
nation, but we have refused. Our leaders have turned down the
opportunity to repent and have received the just consequences
from a mighty God.

The enemies of America, jihadist Islam and progressive
atheism, unleashed an attack on America in 2001 which was
the last medicinal judgment for America. On Tuesday
morning, September 11, 2001 a friend called me and said,
"Turn on your TV; something bad is happening." I tuned into
the news just in time to see the second plane slam into the
Twin Towers in New York City. It was the last medicinal judgment of God on America. We had been given time to repent
of our Immorality, Idolatry, and killing Innocents, and we did
not do it. We had given only lip service to everything God
requires of a nation that needs to repent.

In September 2001, we had committed the three transgressions, and the cup was full—but we weren't quite at the
end of God's rope. That point came in 2004. As I will explain
in Chapter 4, that's when we crossed over the line, and I
believe we are now done with medicinal judgments from God.
We have violated our obligation to honor God's laws and will
face the consequences.

All nations are obligated to obey the laws of nature established by the Sovereign of the Universe. These laws have been
downloaded into the hearts of people and as a result, God
expects people to follow them. We should not be surprised
that, as God designed the world to be made up of nations, He
also established universal norms for behavior. These laws are
self-evident, as Romans 1:19 and 2:14-15 make plain:

> [T]hat which is known about God is evident within
> them; for God made it evident to them. . . . For when

Gentiles who do not have the Law do instinctively the things of the Law, these, not having the Law are a law to themselves, in that they show the work of the Law written in their hearts, their conscience bearing witness, and their thoughts alternately accusing or else defending them.

Ironically, individual Christian ethics sometimes conflict with national ethics established by God, and Christians can find themselves advocating for things that God prohibits. The immigration of Muslims from the Middle East into America is an example of this. Out of love, individual Christians will see this as an opportunity to witness to and love their unsaved neighbors, and this attitude is certainly right and good. Unfortunately, it flies in the face of what God also expects of our nation. We must consider the next level of what God requires that our country demand of any alien entering America. Let me pose a series of questions to make the point.

- Do you believe Jesus is the Lord over the nations?
- Do you believe God has made America responsible for the protection of its citizens, according to Romans 13:1-6?
- Do you advocate that Muslims give up Sharia law as their sovereign law and live by our constitution?

Your answers, of course, should be "yes, yes, and yes." If a Muslim will not give up Sharia law as sovereign over his or her life, then he or she should not be allowed into our country—period! Sharia law is incompatible with American law and our constitution. Yet the current trend to allow anyone into America is breaking down our culture and leading to conflict.

That we allow this is another way America is in rebellion against God, and it fits the description of Psalm 2:1-2: "Why are the nations in an uproar and the peoples devising a vain thing? The kings of the earth take their stand and the rulers take counsel together against the Lord and against His Anointed." As the UN and other nations of the world seek more and more to live out the attitudes of this prophecy by taking a stand against God, American Christians must pray for personal clarity on such issues and make sure their beliefs and actions remain thoroughly consistent with the truths that should guide our lives.

In *American Hour*, Os Guinness offers an explanation of how a nation loses its power, and his observation is consistent with what we see happening in the United States today:

> A crisis of cultural authority occurs,when a culture's faiths lose their inner compelling power, either because of a rival faith challenging them or because in changed circumstances they fail to commend a continuing assent from their own adherents.[29]

A rival faith has, indeed, invaded our land, and what once was honored in America is honored no more. The cold reality of our national sins has accumulated to the breaking point over the past half century, and an avalanche is about to occur.

What We Have Learned So Far

1. *Nations without special revelation (the Bible) are judged on general revelation which includes conscience, logic,*

---

29 Guiness, 28.

history, and intuition.

2.   *Nations with special revelation (the Bible) are judged by what God has revealed.*

3.   *Passive judgment from God means that God turns people over to behavior they are wanting and practicing; it leads to natural consequences inherent in the design of creation.*

4.   *America is being judged harshly because she has received special revelation and yet rejected it, refusing to repent.*

5.   *From 1960 to 2004, America fell under medicinal judgments from God which were meant to heal the nation and lead us to repent. Since 2004, though, we have come under a final judgment.*

The 'I' Judgments

4

THE FINAL JUDGMENT ON US

*He rules by His might forever; His eyes keep watch on the nations;
let not the rebellious exalt themselves*—Psalm 66:7

Final judgments come in a variety of sizes and colors. For example, God sent a judgment on Egypt during the Exodus conflict with Israel. Although Egypt continued as a nation, Egypt was fundamentally different after the judgment than it was before the judgment. Pharaoh was dead, the army decimated, the economy in shambles, and the work force of over one million Jews was gone. Life was much harder in Egypt after the destruction wrought by the ten plagues and the death of its leader. Sometimes God's final judgment leaves a country decimated but still able to limp along as a nation.

Other times, a final judgment may bring a complete end to that nation. The book of Obadiah, for instance, tells of the destruction of Edom. Have you heard much about Edom lately? You won't find any representatives at the U.N. from Edom, and there's no Edomite embassy in Washington, D.C.

God had made a promise to Edom: "'Though you build high like the eagle, though you set your nest among the stars, from there I will bring you down,' declares the Lord" (Obadiah 1:4). Even if the Edomites try to rebuild their nation, God is planning to destroy all their efforts. And in Obadiah 1:10, God proclaims this warning: "Because of violence to your brother Jacob, you will be covered with shame, and you will be cut off *forever*" (emphasis mine). God had seen Edom's vicious treatment of her brother, the nation of Israel, and it was intolerable. Edom committed the Israel "I" sin of brother-on-brother hatred.

In addition to the judgment in which a decimated nation continues to exist and the one in which a nation is destroyed for good, there is a third type of final judgment demonstrated in God's treatment of the nation of Israel and her neighbors. In this judgment, God brings down a nation with a promise to bring it back. Jeremiah 12:14-17 describes this type of judgment:

> Thus says the Lord concerning all My wicked neighbors who strike at the inheritance with which I have endowed My people Israel, "Behold I am about to uproot them from their land and will uproot the house of Judah from among them. And it will come about that after I have uprooted them, I will again have compassion on them; and I will bring them back, each one to his inheritance and each one to his land. Then it will come about that if they will really learn the ways of My people, to swear by My name, 'As the Lord lives,' even as they taught My people to swear by Baal, then they will be built up in the midst of My people. But if they will not listen, then I will uproot that nation, uproot and destroy it," declares the Lord.

Notice that God makes a promise to all of the nations surrounding Israel—the ones who had attacked and tried to destroy Israel. The Lord promises to have compassion on them, and He even promises to bring those nations back if they learn what He wants them to.

Lesson Learned?

Countries that have come under judgment must "learn the ways of My people" and "swear by My name." If they do that, then they will be reestablished. All nations are responsible to learn the Ten Commandments and live by them.

God requires the nations to walk in His ways, as described in Psalm 77:13—"Thy way, O God, is holy; what god is great like our God?"—and Psalm 25:4—"Make me know Thy ways, O Lord; teach me Thy paths." The nations have a choice: Choose the way which God points to or choose your own way.

In addition to learning God's ways and living by them, the nations must also learn to "swear by My name" and no longer honor the name of any false god. "Swearing by God's name" means recognizing God as the Creator of the universe. The nations surrounding Israel swore by the name of Baal, and they influenced Israel to do the same. According to the promise, though, if they learn the "ways of My people" and return to swearing by the "name of the Lord," then they will be brought back to their inheritance and be blessed.

To swear by God's name also implies the taking of an oath. Jeremiah 4:2 explains this: "And you will swear, 'As the LORD lives,' In truth, in justice and in righteousness; Then the nations will bless themselves in Him, And in Him they will glory." The significance of this swearing for a nation is that it is a commitment to monotheism under the one God who created the heavens and the earth. This one God is He who guides people into truth, justice, and righteousness. Seeking anything else as the source of truth, justice, and righteousness will lead to a final judgment upon the nation. As Jeremiah 12:17 says, "'But if they will not listen, then I will uproot that nation, uproot and destroy it,' declares the Lord."

Unfortunately for the Edomites, they did not learn their lessons, and as a result, they were destroyed as a nation and have never returned to the world scene. Israel's other wicked neighbors, however, still had a chance, and some lived, but some died. America is like one of the nations that surrounded Israel.

Our Turn to Learn

The United States is unique on the face of the earth. We still "hold these truths to be self-evident, that all men are created equal, that they are endowed by their Creator with certain unalienable rights that among these are Life, Liberty, and the pursuit of Happiness." Or do we?

At the founding of this nation, we acknowledged the Creator God—and not the governments of sinful men—as the Source of our rights. It was clear to the founders that the Continental army could not defeat the armed forces of the British Empire. They believed the founding of this country would be solely the work of Almighty God. The Creator of the heavens and the earth, "Nature's God," would have to be the One who, by His own power and divine will, moved to establish the United States of America. This nation was established on the foundation that the Jewish/Christian God, who is the only God, secured our freedoms because "all men are created equal." Yet even we have severely tested that truth.

Thomas Jefferson, the writer and one of the signers of the Declaration of Independence, said, "I tremble for my country when I reflect that God is just, that His justice cannot sleep forever." This quote is part of a larger quotation on the Jefferson Memorial in Washington, D.C., and panel three of the memorial, provides the full quote and reveals the context of why he was concerned:

> God who gave us life gave us liberty. Can the liberties of a nation be secure when we have removed conviction that these liberties are the gift of God? Indeed I tremble for my nation when I reflect that God is just, that His justice cannot sleep forever. Commerce

between master and slave is despotism. Nothing is more certainly written in the book of fate than that these people are to be free. Establish a law for educating the common people. This it is the business of the state and on a general plan.[30]

The troubling irony, of course, is that Jefferson himself owned more than 200 slaves and, as a slaveholder, embodied every reason why God would send a final judgment on America. Even though Jefferson warned the nation, he did not act on what he knew to be right when it was in his power to do so. Yet God in His grace repeatedly raised up men to warn the nation against slavery. From the writing of the Constitution to the time of the Civil War, the United States made strides in the right direction to abolish slavery. However, the nation did not do what was necessary to abolish slavery without a war. Hence, the Civil War was America's first final judgment.

John Jay, one of our founding fathers, was a Christian and avid reader of the Bible. He helped establish the American Bible Society in order to print and distribute the Scriptures to the American people. His son, William Jay, studied at Yale under the great Bible teacher Timothy Dwight,[31] who was one of the leaders of the Second Great Awakening. Allan Weinreb writes of him:

William became one of America's leading abolitionists, and the foundation of his beliefs was his religious faith. In his words, the anti-slavery cause was, "strictly a religious one, founded on the gospel of Jesus Christ."[32]

---

30 Jefferson Memorial Monument.
31 Allan Weinreb, "The Jays and Religion," October 2010, posted at: http://johnjay-homestead.org/wp-content/uploads/The_Jays_and_Religion_for_website.pdf
32 "The Jays and Religion," 6.

William Jay, like many preachers in that time, felt real anger at southern preachers who defended slavery based on biblical texts. Appalled at the racism in his own denomination, he also fought for a black man, Alexander Crummell, to be admitted to the General Theological Seminary of the Episcopal Church. Crummell was finally admitted to the Episcopal Seminary of Boston, went on to be ordained, and led a black congregation that was eventually accepted into the Episcopal Convention in 1846.

America's battle against slavery was a fight against the four sins of which God says, "If you cross these lines, you will surely receive the wrath of God." The South, in utter rebellion against God, chose to cross those lines. They crossed the line of Idolatry by falsely claiming that the God of the Bible endorsed their enslaving a whole race of people. They denied that their slaves were made in the image of God, and therefore, they denied the Bible. They crossed the Immorality line when they treated their slaves as property and gave rights to slave owners to use the bodies of their slaves for whatever they wanted, including sexually immoral behavior. They crossed the line of Innocents when they killed innocent slaves. And they crossed the line of Israel by their racist denial of a people's rights under God.

The South even went so far as to set up their own government which God destroyed. To bring a final judgment on this people, God raised up a leader for America who could guide the nation through the terrible time of wrath and who came to understand the Lord's will for the nation. Abraham Lincoln understood better than most that the judgment from God was on the whole nation, both North and South, and that no one was innocent.

In Lincoln's Second Inaugural Address, the President offered a biblical understanding of how God judges nations. He was a Bible-reading man who believed in our Lord, and his ideas are important to us today as we face the wrath of God once again in our nation. On March 4, 1865, Lincoln gave the speech that included these momentous words:

Neither party expected for the war the magnitude or the duration which it has already attained. Neither anticipated that the cause of the conflict might cease with or even before the conflict itself should cease. Each looked for an easier triumph, and a result less fundamental and astounding. Both read the same Bible and pray to the same God, and each invokes His aid against the other.

It may seem strange that any men should dare to ask a just God's assistance in wringing their bread from the sweat of other men's faces, but let us judge not, that we be not judged. The prayers of both could not be answered. That of neither has been answered fully. The Almighty has His own purposes. "Woe unto the world because of offenses; for it must needs be that offenses come, but woe to that man by whom the offense cometh."

If we shall suppose that American slavery is one of those offenses which, in the providence of God, must needs come, but which, having continued through His appointed time, He now wills to remove, and that He gives to both *North* and *South* this terrible war as the woe due to those by whom the offense came, shall we discern therein any departure from those divine attributes which the believers in a living God always ascribe to Him? Fondly do we hope, fervently do we pray, that this mighty scourge of war may speedily pass away. Yet, if God wills that it continue until all the wealth piled by the bondsman's two hundred and fifty years of unrequited toil shall be sunk, and until every drop of blood drawn with the lash shall be paid by another drawn with the sword, as was said three thousand years ago, so still it must be said "the judgments of the Lord are true and righteous altogether."[33] (emphasis mine)

John Wilkes Booth assassinated Lincoln just five days after General Robert E. Lee surrendered his Confederate Army to General Grant, ending the Civil War. God destroyed the Southern Confederacy, her government, economy, cities, people, and its institution of slavery. Her government lasted less than five years, ultimately destroyed by the living God, not by the Union Army. Thus, President Lincoln understood better than most that, "the judgments of the Lord are true; they are righteous altogether" (Psalm 19:9).

President Lincoln quoted from Matthew 18:7 which says, "Woe to the world because of its stumbling blocks! For it is inevitable that stumbling blocks come; but woe to that man through whom the stumbling block comes!" The term stumbling block literally means a snare or a trap. God in His providence sets certain tests, teachings, or desires before nations to cause its people to make a decision. Every such decision leads either to the way of righteousness or to the way of wickedness. Slavery became a snare for America which tested the very fabric of our values, traditions, and deepest beliefs.

Once again, America is being tested, and frankly, I do not think we are up to facing a final judgment from the Lord. In 1860, America was a different country, full of churches and preachers. Every school used the Bible as a textbook, and

---

33 Lincoln's Second Inaugural Address, http://en.wikipedia.org/wiki/Abraham_Lincoln%27s_second_inaugural_address

people generally acknowledged the Judeo-Christian world-view and ethic. Obviously, that is no longer true. We no longer have the basic moral consensus of early American society, and one extremely important factor in this lack of consensus is that we are no longer a nation that fears God.

The importance of "fearing God" shows up in the very first book of the Bible. In Genesis 20, Abraham caused a problem with King Abimelech when he claimed that his wife was his sister. He did it because there was "no fear of God in this place" (vs. 11). "Fear" means either reverence or being afraid. Yet God commands that all people fear Him. Without the fear of God, a people group has no constraints on what they might do. Abraham recognized that Abimilech's people had no sense of accountability to anyone higher than themselves, and it terrified him.

America today is like the nation of Abimilech. If Abraham were here, he would fear us because there is no fear of God.

By contrast, 2 Samuel 23:3 reflects the right attitude of a leader toward God: "The God of Israel said, the Rock of Israel spoke to me, 'He who rules over men righteously, who rules in the fear of God.'" David is talking about his own rule and how God wants all nations to be ruled by those who fear God. As Americans, we need to learn again how to fear the Lord. Now that we have crossed over the four "I" sin milestones, Christians need to talk more about the fear of God. We need to look at our own lives and "up our game" on fearing God in these days that are so similar to the days of Noah and Lot! Our nation's leaders need to hear more from the people and let increased fear of God heal our nation. If you'd like to study more about the fear of God, I recommend that you read Jerry Bridges' excellent book, *The Joy of Fearing God*.

An overview of historical patterns also suggests a timing

that does not bode well for contemporary America. Alexander Tyler, a professor of history at the University of Edinburgh in the eighteenth century, is generally quoted as the source of this remarkable observation about democratic societies:

> A democracy is always temporary in nature; it simply cannot exist as a permanent form of government. A democracy will continue to exist up until the time that voters discover that they can vote themselves generous gifts from the public treasury. From that moment on, the majority always votes for the candidates who promise the most benefits from the public treasury, with the result that every democracy will finally collapse due to loose fiscal policy which is always followed by a dictatorship. The average age of the world's greatest civilizations from the beginning of history has been about 200 years. During those 200 years, these nations always progressed through the following sequence: from bondage to spiritual faith, from spiritual faith to great courage, from courage to liberty, from liberty to abundance, from abundance to selfishness, from selfishness to complacency, from complacency to apathy, from apathy to dependence, from dependence back to bondage.[34]

During the Civil War, our young nation was at the courage-to-liberty phase in the cycle of nations. Our president was seeking the Lord, and his speeches were full of godly wisdom as he often quoted Scripture.

Lincoln's Second Inaugural Address is a gift to America because God, in His providence, taught the nation important

---

34 Alexander Tyler, Wikipedia, posted at https://en.wikipedia.org/wiki/Alexander_Fraser_Tytler

truths which we are in dire need of following now. First, the speech explained that God is on His own side, not on the side of the North or the South (or, by implication, any other people group). Lincoln affirmed that "the Almighty has His own purposes" and that, "in the providence of God, [slavery] must needs come, but which having continued through His appointed time, He now wills to remove, and that He gives to both North and South this terrible war as the woe due to those by whom the offense cameth."[35]

God exerts His own purposes for nations, and their rising and falling are completely in His hand. America seems to think that only blessing should follow good behavior, while Lincoln claimed that the North, despite its opposition to slavery, nevertheless was due a share of the suffering. And suffer it did! The North alone lost more than 300,000 men in the war. Can you imagine the heartache and pain that so many families had to endure? The lesson is a hard one but must be learned: The righteous will suffer along with the unrighteous when God sends His wrath.

Jeremiah endured pain and suffering because of the judgment God brought to Judah and Jerusalem. The prophet Ezekiel was taken into captivity, and Daniel was whisked off to the palace of the king of Babylon. The righteous have always suffered along with the unrighteous when a nation is under God's judgment.

In 2016, as I write this book, America is at the same place it was in 1860. We face a final judgment. As I catalogue for you exactly why that is, please have the attitude of our brother and forefather, Abraham Lincoln, as he accepted the ways of our sovereign, loving God.

---

35 Lincoln's Second Inaugural Address.

American Idols

Since 1963, our nation has pursued an idolatrous relationship with false gods. We have rewritten history so as to exclude God from any part of our founding or to deny the blessings which He bestowed on us.

Two events happened in 1962 and 1963 that fundamentally changed America. In 1962, the Supreme Court, in *Engle v. Vitale*, ruled that it was unconstitutional for state officials to compose an official prayer and encourage its recitation in public schools. The "sinister" prayer that brought the case before the court was: "Almighty God, we acknowledge our dependence upon Thee and we beg Thy blessings upon us, our parents, our teachers and our country, Amen." This ruling set the modern Supreme Court into conflict with our founders, who had called for fasting and prayer before writing the Declaration of Independence, as well as before hundreds of other official acts of the government. The 1962 Court was also in conflict with President Franklin Roosevelt, who wrote a prayer and put it into a Bible to give to all U.S. servicemen going off to World War II. Essentially, our whole history and national identity was denied by the wicked and unrighteous judges on the 1962 Supreme Court.

To make matters worse, the very next year, the Supreme Court ruled in *Murray v. Curlett* that school-sponsored Bible reading in public schools was *unconstitutional.* Now prayer and the Bible were persona non grata in the public schools of America. The Court handed down its ruling on June 17, 1963, five months before President Kennedy was shot and killed. Many will scoff at the idea that, in the supernatural or the providence of God, there is a connection between the two, but, believe me, there is! Just as President Kennedy was having multiple affairs with other women, breaking the covenant with his wife, so America was having her own affairs with false gods.

Once the nation established in law that she was getting rid of God so she could have her affairs, two other striking things happened: The sexual revolution and the de facto removal of the First Amendment from the Constitution. The sexual revolution brought us broken families and untold disasters for children. The statistics about this are undeniable, so I will not belabor the point, but the resulting brokenness is its own judgment from God. Colossians 3:5-6 says:

> Therefore consider the members of your earthly body as dead to immorality, impurity, passion, evil desire, and greed, which amount to idolatry. For it is because of these things that the wrath of God will come upon the sons of disobedience.

The speed of the media, Hollywood, universities, and businesses in pursuing the idol of sex and the flesh is astounding. As Colossians 3 points out, this idolatry leads to the wrath of God, and since 1963, America has been experiencing God's passive wrath. God gave America over to sins of the flesh, and we have been receiving our due ever since. The second movement that started during the same period of time, however, may be even more deadly.

The movement to drive out the truths of the First Amendment and destroy them is a direct result of our pursuit of idolatry. To refresh your memory, the First Amendment says that:

> Congress shall make no law respecting an establishment of religion, or prohibiting the free exercise thereof; or abridging the freedom of speech, or of the press; or

the right of the people peaceably to assemble, and to petition the Government for a redress of grievances.

Nevertheless, courts have assaulted Christianity, trying to eliminate any practice or belief from the public square.

"Reinterpreting" the First Amendment is an attempt to eradicate any Christian influence on America. Our forefathers would be ashamed and horrified at the lying and deception of the judges who assert meanings to the First Amendment that were never intended. These evil judges rule that "no establishment of religion" means that government must eliminate Christianity and that "free exercise thereof" means you can exercise your religion only in your own mind or church.

To demonstrate the extreme this has reached: Pastor Erwin Lutzer tells of a girl who wore a chastity bracelet at school because she was committed to remain a virgin until marriage. Her high school banned the bracelet, though, because it was "deemed religious."[36] I never thought that in my lifetime the United States would be closer to the Soviet Union than to the America of the Constitution, but our courts have effectively driven Christianity out of the public square, and I fear that Christians will soon end up in jail for their beliefs.

Killing Innocence, Killing Innocents

Pursuit of idols always leads to murder. Once the courts began to destroy our freedom of religion and the sexual revolution deprived us of our innocence, the courts moved on to fabricate a law protecting the right of some people to murder others. In 1973, America crossed the killing Innocents line when it established in law that a woman has the right to abort

---

36 Erwin W. Lutzer, *Is God on America's Side?: The Surprising Answer and How It Affects Our Future.* (Chicago: Moody Publishers, 2008), 12.

her unborn baby. Since then, America has killed more than 56 million children. If God was willing to avenge slavery in America by killing over 600,000 of our citizens in the Civil War, I tremble to think of what we are due to right the wrong of abortion.

As an American, you need to pray for mercy, because Numbers 35:33 *will be fulfilled* in our nation. The scripture says, "So you shall not pollute the land in which you are; for blood pollutes the land and no expiation can be made for the land for the blood that is shed on it, except by the blood of him who shed it." This passage establishes a principle by which God has judged many nations. Shedding innocent blood is an abomination to God and a disgrace to a nation. Just as the abolitionist movement in the 1800s could not prevent the Civil War from coming, so the pro-life movement will not prevent God from bringing His wrath on the nation for murdering so many children. We have a blood debt with God, and it will be paid. In Numbers 35:33, the word *expiation* means *cover* or *atonement*, and since the passage promises no expiation, we will have no protection from the wrath of God!

Many people shrug their shoulders at an idea such as God venting His wrath on a nation. This is because we have greatly reduced our estimation of who God is. R. C. Sproul says America's view of God today is that, "He is a deity without sovereignty, a god without wrath, a judge without judgment, and a force without power."[37] It is beyond alarming to see the level of defection and traitorous behavior with which America has treated the God of the Bible, the sovereign God who raised up this nation in 1776. Erwin Lutzer notes that "God judges nations based on the amount of light and opportunity they are given."[38] Does anyone doubt that America has had

37 Cited in Lutzer, 13.
38 Ibid., 17.

more light and opportunity than any nation on the planet? To turn Idolatry and killing Innocents into national laws is the most blatant possible rebellion against God, our history, and our forefathers.

As we wrap up this discussion of killing Innocents, let me make some historical ties to the Supreme Court abortion decision. Spiro Agnew, vice president during the Watergate scandal, resigned from his position on October 10, 1973, and President Nixon resigned on August 9, 1974. Also in October 1973, Israel's Yom Kippur War broke out, and then Prime Minister Golda Meir ordered that thirteen nuclear missles be readied to launch at Syria and Egypt. In response, the Soviets sent nukes to Egypt, and the U.S. prepared for nuclear war. This was a harbinger for what we will face in the future. In the midst of this international turmoil, the Supreme Court handed down the *Roe v. Wade* decision on January 22, 1973. In a 7-2 decision, an astounding majority of court judges ruled in favor of killing Innocents. As a result, America was failing miserably in 1973.

Bringing the connections into the present, in 2015 Planned Parenthood was exposed for selling baby parts from aborted children. The videos that have exposed this evil shined a light on the murder and maiming of babies. Some of the perpetrators even admitted that some babies were alive when their organs were harvested! The videos are so abhorrent that many people I know will not watch them. I can only conclude that the sin of killing Innocents has risen in the cup to the point that God is ready to judge America.

Immoral Is as Immoral Does

I remember sitting in the parking lot of a grocery store on a warm summer day in 2003, reading about a Supreme Court decision that I have come to believe pushed us across the line of Immorality as a nation. On June 26, 2003 in a 6-3 decision, the Supreme Court ruled:

> that homosexuals had a protected liberty to engage in private sexual activity, that homosexuals' moral and sexual choices were entitled to Constitutional protection; and that moral disapproval did not provide a legitimate justification for Texas' law criminalizing sodomy.[39]

This decision set American against American, and Christians will no longer be entitled to their moral objection to homosexuality. They will be persecuted over this issue.

In 2015, the Court furthered this disaster by legalizing gay marriage. As the *New York Times* reported, Justice Kennedy proclaimed that "no longer may this liberty be denied."[40] By a vote of 5-4, the Supreme Court guaranteed a right to same -sex marriage, and it led immediately to the prosecution of Christians for opposing the law.

With the homosexual court rulings, America has three of the four I's written into law. These laws have been maturing and growing, and now America's cup is overflowing with the resultant sins. America has refused to repent and has solidified her desire to preserve these three sins as part of our culture. At the same time, the righteous and moral among us have solidified our conviction that the Ten Commandments remain right and good for America.

The final judgment has been upon America since 2004, and the evidence for it resides in a pattern: With the loss of our freedoms comes the rise of even more laws which enslave

---

39 Wikipedia, *Lawrence v. Texas.*
40 "2015 SCOTUS Decision on *Obergfells vs. Hodges,*" *New York Times.*

us. We are unraveling as a culture, slipping into a society of death, destruction, and fear. Fear of the government has grown exponentially in my lifetime, and disease, war, and disasters have multiplied at an alarming pace. In 1942, America was protected from invading armies by two oceans, but today, we are under the threat of missiles from numerous countries that can deliver biological, chemical, or nuclear weapons to our doorstep.

God has removed the hedge of protection from our nation, so that our enemies have greater access to us. You'll recall that, when God removed the protective hedges from Job's property, Satan inspired the Sabeans to attack and put Job's servants to death. Likewise, his children died, and all that Job owned was destroyed. It should stand as a reminder that the unseen world is ruled by God, and Satan has no authority except what he is given by the Lord. If God puts a protective shield around your nation and her people, nothing will harm them. But if God removes that protective shield, then the nation's enemies have a free hand to attack.

There is an inescapable connection between the seen and unseen world, and America has tried to escape this truth, but to no avail. The more that progressive atheists rule our government, schools, and media, the greater the suffering they will cause as the wrath of God puts increasing pressure on our nation.

Under the judgment of God, America can no longer defend her borders. Since January 2014, more than 300,000 illegal aliens have crossed our southern border, including 50,000 unaccompanied children. Journalist Peggy Noonan wrote a July 11, 2014 op-ed in *Real Clear Politics*, in which she observed that "a nation without a border is no longer a nation." Movies and books have even built on the theme of terrorists infiltrating our border with Mexico and wreaking devastation.

Yet since 2004, we have seen an utter lack of courage and action by our leaders to defend our borders. A nation which will not define its borders or protect them will fall.

Jesus said, "If a kingdom is divided against itself, that kingdom cannot stand" (Mark 3:24). Can anyone doubt that America is divided against itself, and that the author of division, Satan, has free reign in our country? Since 2004, the division between progressive atheists and supporters of a Judeo-Christian republic has grown to a breaking point. Progressives attack the church and true Christians like never before, and soon, everyone will be required to agree with their views— such as toleration of homosexuality—or face criminal charges.

At this point, we must stand fast in the conviction that no true believer in Jesus Christ, no born again believer, will become a traitor to his or her Lord, the King of Kings and the Holy One of Israel. True Christians confront evil, take up their spiritual weapons, and stand firm. When progressive atheists take our jobs, steal our money, or put us in jail, do they really believe we will betray our heavenly Father? I say, "No!" We will be like Job who said, "The Lord gives and the Lord takes away, blessed be the name of the Lord" (Job 1:21).

True believers in the living God are also being attacked by a false church. Many denominations have betrayed the Lord. Episcopalians ordain homosexuals, and Methodists, Lutherans, and Presbyterians have all betrayed the Lord in their own ways. Traitors to the faith even attempt to put pressure on true believers to take up their folly. Yet their just punishment is coming soon. I thank God for congregations that have split from these denominations and taken a stand for the Lord!

There is only one hope for America. We must turn back from our folly and rescind the Supreme Court decisions of 1962, 1963, 1973, 2003, and 2015 or face the wrath of God. There is no other way out of the destruction planned for the

United States. Otherwise, the inevitable destruction will be far worse than the Civil War, the most costly war in our history.

Blind to Our Enemies

If destruction comes, where will it come from? We have many enemies who urgently desire the destruction of this country and who are actively working to remove the USA from the face of the earth. As I said earlier, Iran has held a conference every year since 1979 that touts the destruction of the United States. Iran envisions a world without America or Israel, but we just can't seem to believe they really want that. Princeton professor Bernard Lewis, explained in the documentary film *Iranium* the reluctance of America to believe that anyone wants to kill us:

> There is a certain cultural relativism in the West which makes it reluctant to condemn, particularly to condemn another civilization; we must be nice to them; we must be tolerant and understanding and so forth. But this must not go to the level of blinding ourselves to the more painful realities of the situation.[41]

In saying this, Professor Lewis has put his finger on one of the judgments of God on America: God has given us eyes to see, but we cannot see! After 35 years of state-sponsored terrorism, we still treat Iran as if it can be trusted, even to the point that we sign treaties with the abhorrent nation. Even though Iran's leaders preach that they will kill every Jew on the planet, we welcome them to New York to speak at the United Nations. Iran's leaders boast that they will finish the job Hitler started, to kill every Jew—including those living

---

41 From the movie, *Iranium.*

in the United States. Yet our government refuses to stand up and protect these Americans, and a government that refuses to appropriately protect some of its citizens will eventually refuse to protect any of them.

If America will not keep Iranian leaders from preaching their hate-filled, anti-American, anti-Semitic messages even within our borders, then America is too weak to protect her citizens. We are blind to the enemies and attacks which assault us and too weak to respond. From the other side of the world, China attacks our computers every day through state-sponsored theft, destruction, and hatred of our nation and land, but our response increasingly seems to be too little and too late.

Perhaps one of the most intriguing critiques of our present situation comes from Niall Ferguson, author of *Civilization, the West and the Rest.* In his book, Ferguson explains, "what distinguished the West from the rest—the mainsprings of global power—were six identifiable novel complexes of institutions and associated ideas and behaviors."[42] He calls these six ideas the "killer apps" that "allowed a minority of mankind originating on the western edge of Eurasia to dominate the world for the better part of 500 years." The six killer apps are competition, science, property rights, medicine, the consumer society, and the work ethic. Perhaps the most startling indictment in the book is Ferguson's critique of Christians in America. Referring to Max Weber and Adam Smith who saw the tie between the Protestant work ethic and the economic success that America experienced, Ferguson says:

> Yet there is something about today's American Evangelicals that would have struck Weber, if not Smith

---

42 Niall Ferguson, *Civilization: The West and the Rest* (New York: Penguin, 2011), 12.

as suspect. For there is a sense in which many of the most successful sects today flourish precisely because they have developed a kind of consumer Christianity that verges on Walmart worship.[43]

When the Church is that weak, it foreshadows disaster for the nation.

What We Have Learned So Far

1. *There are three forms of final judgment:*

   - *A nation is decimated but continues;*

   - *A nation is totally destroyed and removed from history;*

   - *A nation is punished but brought back if it will "learn the ways of My people" and will "swear by My name" (i.e., take an oath to monotheism and the Creator God).*

2. *America experienced a final judgment from God in the Civil War. The government of the South was completely destroyed.*

3. *The Second Inaugural Address of Lincoln teaches that God will bring judgment on His own sovereign terms.*

4. *The righteous will suffer with the unrighteous.*

5. *God will fulfill the truths of Numbers 35:33 and shed the blood of those who kill innocents.*

---

43 Ibid., 276.

6. *God has removed His protective hedges from our nation.*

THE 'I' JUDGMENTS

5

CRITICAL TIMES WITH ISRAEL

Hear the word of the Lord, O nations,
and declare in the coastlands afar off, and say,
"He who scattered Israel will gather him and keep him
as a shepherd keeps his flock."—Jeremiah 31:10

On May 14, 1948, Israel became a nation again for the first time in nearly nineteen hundred years. Since 70 A.D., Israel had been scattered among the nations, but international agreements after World Wars I and II allowed Israel to become a sovereign state. This is all the more thrilling because, since 586 B.C., Gentile nations have held sovereignty over the land of Israel. Even when considered a "country," Israel fell under a succession of powers including Babylon, Persia, Greece, and Rome. And after 70 A.D., the land itself remained under "foreign" control all the way through the demise of the Ottoman Empire in the early twentieth century. Beginning in 1948, though, this subjection to Gentile power ended. Jeremiah 30-33 describes the change which came to the nations.

In Jeremiah 31:10 (see chapter opening), God describes in one verse why all the nations of the world should care that Israel is back in her land. The message clearly is intended for the nations of the world when God says, "Hear the word of the Lord, O *nations*" (emphasis mine). The prophetic announcement refers to an extraordinary time in history when God gathers Israel into her land. God makes this point strongly when He adds this phrase, "and declare in the coastlands afar off." When God says hear and declare, all nations should perk up because God has a significant message. The events and wonders God has prepared for the nations begin when God brings Israel back to the land.

Scatter and Gather—Repeat as Necessary

The message of Jeremiah 31:10 is about two important issues. God makes a promise when He says, "He who scattered Israel will gather him." God scattered Israel in 721 B.C. when the Assyrians invaded Israel, the ten tribes that made up the northern confederacy. God furthered the disaster in 586 B.C. when Judah and Jerusalem were destroyed by the Babylonians. Seventy years later, after a remnant came back to the land under the Persians, Israel existed as a vassal state, without king or prince, always under the sovereignty of another power. In 70 A.D., the Romans destroyed Israel and scattered her further.

This history of scattering underscores the significance of God's promise that "He who scattered Israel will gather her." It provides evidence that God is working among the nations. And notice that the scattering was literally fulfilled. This is not figurative language. The Jewish people had been physically removed from their land and had to find new homes among various nations. So, if the scattering is literal history, then the logical reading of the passage would conclude that the gathering is literal as well. This is the theme of chapters 30 to 33 in Jeremiah. A series of verses shows how this prophetic drama will play out.

- Jeremiah 30:3—"'For behold, days are coming,' declares the Lord, 'when I will restore the fortunes of My people Israel and Judah.' The Lord says, 'I will also bring them back to the land that I gave to their forefathers and they shall possess it.'" (For 2,500 years Israel did not possess their land the way their forefathers Joshua, Samuel, and

David did, but on May 14, 1948, things changed.)

- Jeremiah 32:37—"Behold, I will gather them out of all the lands to which I have driven them in My anger, in My wrath, and in great indignation; and I will bring them back to this place and make them dwell in safety."

- Jeremiah 32:41—"And I will rejoice over them to do them good, and will faithfully plant them in this land with all My heart and with all My soul."

- Jeremiah 33:6-7—"Behold, I will bring to it health and healing, and I will heal them; and I will reveal to them an abundance of peace and truth. And I will restore the fortunes of Judah and the fortunes of Israel and will rebuild them as they were at first."

God is emphatic about what He is going to do and what His attitude is while He does it. He will show and is showing great love toward the Jewish nation to bring them back and give them safety. They were never truly safe in the "scattering" phase of this prophecy. So doesn't it seem strange that churches and nations are angry at the Jews because they have a safe place where they can defend themselves? The history of churches and nations are stained by the shedding of Jewish blood. What a tragedy!

These excerpts from Jeremiah 30-33 are key examples of the Lord's promise about gathering Israel, but this promise is also repeated by other prophets. For instance:

- Isaiah 11:11-12—"Then it will happen on that day that the Lord will again recover the second time with His hand the remnant of His people, who will remain, from Assyria, Egypt, Pathros, Cush, Elam, Shinar, Hamath, and from the islands of the sea. And He will lift up a standard for the nations and assemble the banished ones of Israel, and will gather the dispersed of Judah from the four corners of the earth."

- Ezekiel 37:21—"And say to them, 'Thus says the Lord God, "Behold, I will take the sons of Israel from among the nations where they have gone, and I will gather them from every side and bring them into their own land."'"

- Amos 9:14-15—"'Also I will restore the captivity of My people Israel, and they will rebuild the ruined cities and live in them, they will also plant vineyards and drink their wine, and make gardens and eat their fruit. I will also plant them on their land, and they will not again be rooted out from their land which I have given them,' says the Lord your God."

- Zephaniah 3:20—"'At that time I will bring you in, even at the time when I gather you together; indeed, I will give you renown and praise among all the peoples of the earth, when I restore your fortunes before your eyes,' says the Lord."

- Zechariah 10:6—"And I shall strengthen the house of Judah, and I shall save the house of Joseph, and I will bring them back, because I have had compassion on them; and they will be as though I had not rejected them, for I am the Lord their God, and I will answer them."

In our time, God has brought back His chosen nation into

the land of their forefathers, and yet the nations are resisting this providential move of God. They treat Israel with anger, hatred, and threats. These nations would do well to heed the second part of Jeremiah 31:10 which says God will "keep him as a shepherd keeps his flock." God is keeping Israel today, leading the nation as a shepherd leads the flock.

In 1867, theologian J. C. Ryle wrote about this passage from Jeremiah. In his book *Are You Ready for the End of Time?*, Ryle points out, "We ourselves are among the nations to whom Jeremiah speaks. Upon us devolves a portion of the duty which He here sets forth. The text is the Lord's voice to all the churches of Christ among the Gentiles."[44] Now that Israel has been in her land for 67 years, should not the nations rejoice over her and assist her in the work of the Lord? If God is shepherding them, should not the churches of the living God show love to this people? Ryle continues:

> For many centuries there has prevailed in the churches of Christ a strange, and to my mind, an unwarrantable mode of dealing with the word "Israel." It has been interpreted in many passages of the Psalms and Prophets, as if it meant nothing more than Christian believers.[45]

J. C. Ryle is the exception among Christians. Too many have treated the Jews in terrible ways during their scattering phase. Ryle was part of a group of pastors who reached out to the Jews in an evangelistic enterprise, having the same love for them as Paul had in Romans 9 when he said:

> I am telling the truth in Christ, I am not lying, my

---

44 J.C. Ryle, *Are You Ready for the End of Times?* (Christian Heritage, 1969), 97.
45 Ibid., 99.

conscience bearing me witness in the Holy Spirit, that I have great sorrow and unceasing grief in my heart. For I could wish that I myself were accursed, separated from Christ for the sake of my brethren, my kinsmen according to the flesh, who are Israelites. (vv. 1-4a)

According to this passage and Romans 11:1-2, God has not rejected His people.

Christians in Conflict over Israel

Unfortunately for churches, there are two groups clashing with each other: Those who hold that national Israel has not forfeited grace and election, and those who believe that the Church has replaced Israel. Those who teach that the Church has replaced Israel believe that the unconditional promises given to Abraham concerning the land do not apply to Israel.

John Calvin and C. H. Spurgeon are two great teachers in the history of the church who reflect these positions. Both wrote commentaries and preached great sermons, and both were greatly used of the Lord. But look at their differences regarding Israel in their commentaries on Jeremiah 32:41—"I will rejoice over them to do them good and will faithfully plant them in this land with all My heart and with all My soul":

- John Calvin—"Let us then know that the Church was planted in Judea, for it remained to the time of Christ. And as Christ has pulled down the wall of partition, so that there is now no difference between Jews and Gentiles, God plants us now in the holy land when He grafts us into the body of Christ."[46]

- Charles Spurgeon—"We cannot help looking for the restoration of the scattered Israelites to the land which God has given to them by a covenant of salt: We also look for the time when they shall believe in the Messiah who they have rejected and shall rejoice in Jesus of Nazareth, whom today they despise. There is great encouragement in prophecy to those who work among the seed of Israel... Let those who believe work on! Those who believe not may give it up. They shall not have the honor of helping to gather together the ancient nation to which our Lord Himself belonged; for be it never forgotten that Jesus was a Jew."[47]

These two commentaries are typical of the battle which has come down to us. On the one side are those who disregard the territorial promises God gave to Israel and therefore attack the Jews. Consider pastors in the fourth century A.D. like Ambrose of Milan who declared, "'that the Jewish synagogue was a house of impiety, a receptacle of folly, which God Himself has condemned.' Not surprisingly, he [Ambrose] orchestrated and praised the burning of synagogues."[48] Also, John Chrysostom:

The golden mouthed expositor, nevertheless became the most notorious and rabid proponent of anti-Judaism in his generation. In a series of eight homilies

---

46 Cited in Barry E. Horner, *Future Israel: Why Christian Anti-Judaism Must Be Challenged* (Nashville: B&H Academic, 2004), 7.
47 Ibid., 13.
48 Ibid., 20.

against the Jews, his tirade knew no limits, he said, "the synagogues of the Jews are the homes of idolatry and devils even though they have not images in them. They are worse even than heathen circuses. I hate the Jews for they have the law and they insult it."[49]

Over the past 1900 years, men like these have led the church to persecute and murder the Jews, even claiming that Jesus—the greatest Jew who ever lived—wanted Christians to kill the Jews. What a horrible testimony for the church! It only proves a point, though: The theology of those who deny the promises God made to Israel, based on covenantal love and election, is bad theology because it produced bad fruit. Bad theology produces bad fruit, and good theology produces good fruit. In twentieth century America, the same hatred appears again.

Albertus Pieters (1897-1987), who taught at Western Theological Seminary in Holland, Michigan for the Reformed Church in America, said, "God willed that after the institution of the New Covenant there should no longer be any Jewish people in the world yet here they are! That is a fact, a very sad fact, brought about by their rebellion against God." And, "God is through with the Jews."[50]

Loraine Boettner (1901-1990), a member in the Orthodox Presbyterian Church and a graduate of Princeton Theological Seminary, penned *The Reformed Doctrine of Predestination* in which he said:

With the establishment of the Christian Church, Judaism should have made a smooth and willing transition into Christianity, and should thereby have disap-

---

49 Ibid., 21.
50 Ibid., 37-38.

peared as the flower falls away before the developing fruit. Its continued existence as a bitter rival and ene- my of the Christian Church after the time of Christ, and particularly its revival after the judgment of God had fallen on it so heavily in the destruction of Jeru- salem and the dispersal of the people in 70 A.D. was sinful.[51]

What is so terrible about this attitude is that it treats as sinful what is actually glorious! These people, whom God promised to keep together, however improbable that might seem, are treated in hateful and wicked ways. Is it not a mir- acle that a scattered people, with no geographical area to call their own, was nevertheless kept together by the providential hand of God? Beottner goes on to say:

It may seem harsh to say that, "God is through with the Jews." But the fact of the matter is that He is through with them as a unified national group. ... This does not mean, of course, that the Jews will never go back to Palestine—as indeed some of them have al- ready established the nation of Israel, a little less than 2 million out of an estimated world Jewish population of 12 million now being in that country. But it does mean that as any of them go back they do so entirely on their own, apart from any covenanted purpose to that end and entirely outside of Scripture prophecy. No Scripture blessing is promised for a project of that kind.[52]

Considering that Beottner wrote a book on predestination, it

---

51 Loraine Boettner, *The Reformed Doctrine of Predestination,* (Grand Rapids: Eerd- mans, 1954), 41.
52 Ibid., 43.

is incredible that he can deny that the nation of Israel could rise without the aid of Almighty God. This conflict about Israel has serious repercussions on how Christians treat the Jews.

In the June 2014 *Commentary* magazine, Melanie Phillips wrote an article called, "Jesus Was a Palestinian—The Return of Christian Anti-Semitism" in which she argued that millions of evangelicals who support the nation of Israel have been targeted by those who are hostile to the State of Israel. She noted "that religious belief has turned Christian Zionists themselves into a key target for evangelization on the part of those churches that have Israel in their crosshairs."[53] The churches which she mentions are the "Presbyterian Church USA, United Church of Christ, United Methodist, Episcopal Church, and the Evangelical Lutheran Church in America— have legitimized the increasingly virulent anti-Israel movement in the United States."[54] This movement in the churches to divest, boycott, and sanction Israel is part of a larger group of organizations dedicated to the destruction of Israel.

This is the Israel "I" which will turn the Lord's anger against a group or country. Whenever people target Jews, whether individually or corporately for persecution and destruction, you can be sure they will be judged by God.

God, of course, moves ahead with His plans regardless of "Christian" opposition. Jeremiah 30:11 says:

> "For I am with you, "declares the Lord, "to save you; for I will destroy completely all the nations where I have scattered you, only I will not destroy you completely. But I will chasten you justly and will by no means leave you unpunished."

---

53 Melanie Phillips, "Jesus Was a Palestinian-The Return of Christian Anti-Semitism" *Commentary*. June 2014.
54 Ibid., 13.

Clearly, God has chastened His chosen nation the last 2,000 years, and yet, the promise stands that God will destroy nations such as Russia, Germany, and France by whom Jews have been scattered and persecuted. Now the question becomes: Is America one of those nations?

America against the Jews—and God?

Historically, America has been a safe harbor for Jewish people. For instance, in a letter dated August 17, 1790, President Washington wrote to the Sephardic Congregation of Newport, Rhode Island:

> May the children of the stock of Abraham who dwell in the land continue to merit and enjoy the goodwill of the other inhabitants. While everyone shall sit safely under his own vine and fig tree and there shall be none to make him afraid.

Only about 2,000 Jews lived in America at the time Washington wrote his letter, but it generally reflects the tone of America's attitude toward Jews. Certainly, we have never perpetrated the horrible anti-Semitic episodes that have plagued Europe. In fact, many of Europe's Jews have escaped death by fleeing to America.

The pogroms in Europe—and especially Russia—were the reason many Jews came to America. Fleeing persecution in the 1880s, nearly 50,000 Jews immigrated from Russia, Poland, Ukraine, and Romania. By 1924, two million Jews had arrived in the U.S., and today nearly six million Jews live in America—for the most part, in peace and security, even though limited anti-Semitism has been linked to groups like the Ku Klux Klan and neo-Nazi movements. Other anti-Semitic movements have cropped up from time to time as well. During World War II, for instance, these ugly movements arose against American Jews:

> Father Charles E. Coughlin was a Catholic priest whose radio program promoted an anti-Semitic message. Coughlin's Christian Front, organized in 1938, excluded Jews from membership and drew from the most ungodly of the Catholic and Protestant population. Chapter meetings turned into drinking fests, praising Coughlin and cursing the Jews and their leader, Franklin Delano "Rosenfeld." Gangs of these drunken bullies beat up Jews and organized "buy Christian only" campaigns.[55]

Before the war, Coughlin boasted 15 million radio listeners. Once America entered the war, though, many of the anti-Semites had to curtail their behavior or go underground. Finally, in 1942, the Roman Catholic Church "silenced Coughlin on the eve of government action against him."[56] Coughlin, though, blamed the Jews for shutting him down.

> Fritz Kuhn and his German-American Bund was another anti-Semitic organization. Fritz Kuhn was a leader in the Nazi movement in America and drew as many as 25,000 people to some of his rallies. "While on the payroll as a chemist for the Ford Motor Company, Fritz Kuhn, leader of the German-American Bund, was allowed time off to travel around the country espousing the fascist cause."[57]

---

55 David A. Rausch, *A Legacy of Hatred: Why Christians Must Not Forget the Holocaust* (Chicago: Moody Publishers, 1984), 99-100.
56 Ibid., 100.
57 Ibid., 97.

The Bund circulated anti-Semitic materials, had a national radio program, and sponsored retreats and rallies all designed to support and advance the cause of Nazism. Henry Ford was a well-known anti-Semite who supported these causes. In fact, "between 1933 and 1940 more than 120 organizations were actively disseminating anti-Semitic propaganda."[58]

David Rausch, author of *A Legacy of Hatred*, makes a penetrating observation about the 1940s and World War II when he observes:

[T]he fundamentalist-evangelical movement has traditionally been a firm supporter of the Jewish people and has staunchly opposed anti-Semitism. During the Holocaust, Conservative Christians tended to believe that the Jewish people were being exterminated, while more liberal Christians were labeling the reports atrocity propaganda."[59]

Unfortunately, anti-Semitic trends are increasing. Several sources suggest there is a movement in America toward anti-Semitism. While neo-Nazi groups grow in Europe again, America is being influenced by Islam and churches bent on attacking the Jews. The Islamic Society of North America, for example, is:

A sister organization of [CAIR, the Council on American Islamic Relations] with interlocking boards of directors and proven ties to terrorism and murder. Most of their senior members are from the

58 Ibid., 98.
59 Ibid., 103.

Brothers [Muslim Brotherhood]. Shockingly, they are also American citizens, professionals, scholars, doctors, many with PhD's, that give them a veneer of respectability. In *Mafia*, Gaubatz and Sperry wrote, "FBI agents who listened in on their private conversations report they talk about murder and killing Jews, like they were ordering pizza."[60]

This desire to kill all of the Jews in the world is standard thinking in the Muslim world, including Iran, Hezbollah, Hamas, Islamic Jihad, Al Qaeda, Saudi Arabia, and the Muslim Brotherhood. Just as America was infected in the 1930s and 1940s by the Nazis, so today we are infected with the ideology of Islamic Jihad.

Larry Kelley teaches that Immutable Law #9 for fallen civilizations is "When a civilization accepts the propaganda of its enemy as truth, it has reached the far side of appeasement and capitulation is nigh."[61] This is not only happening in American culture, but it is also happening in the churches. Churches are turning against the Jews and those who support them. What is truly strange about this movement is that the very people who want churches to become anti-Semitic are the same ones who would kill Christians if the opportunity arose. Islamic groups that wish to kill the Jews ultimately want Christians dead, too. According to TheReligionofPeace.com, Muslim terrorists—either groups or state-sponsored—murdered 1,033 Christians from a variety of churches and countries in 2014.

The March 2014 GatestoneInstitute.org newsletter featured an article by Raymond Ibrahim, entitled, "Obama Administration Suppresses Talk of Muslim Persecution of

60 Larry Kelley, *Lessons from Fallen Civilizations: Can a Bankrupt America Survive the Current Islamic Threat?* (Englewood, CO: Hugo House, 2012), 280.
61 Ibid., 33.

Christians." In it, Ibrahim catalogues the persecution of the Christians and also those in the American government who suppress and harass anyone who dares to bring up the subject. Here are some examples:

> *Egypt.* During pro-Muslim Brotherhood riots, a young Coptic woman named Mary was murdered simply because her cross identified her as a Christian to Brotherhood rioters.
>
> *Nigeria.* A Muslim father allegedly slaughtered or had someone else slaughter his daughter with a machete, wounding a pastor and four others in the attack, because she had earlier converted to Christianity. Separately, Muslim Fulani herdsmen launched another night raid into a Christian majority region. They massacred over 150 people, including a pastor, his wife and children; around 200 homes were torched.
>
> *Pakistan.* A young Christian girl was killed by Pakistani Taliban in the northern region.
>
> *Somalia.* Members of the militant Islamic group, Al-Shabaal, publicly beheaded a mother of two girls and her cousin after discovering they were Christians.[62]

Later the same year, Charisma News noted that "President Barak Obama was criticized by human rights activists for not addressing the plight of Christians and other minorities during his talk with leaders in Saudi Arabia, where Christianity is actively banned."[63] And when the U.S. State Department blocked a Christian governor from Nigeria from coming to the United States, Emmanuel Ogebe, a Nigerian human rights lawyer based in Washington, D.C., said, "The Christian gov-

---

62 GatestoneInstitute.org, March 2014 Newsletter.
63 GatestoneInstitute.org/4400/obama-muslim-persecutions

ernor's 'visa problems' are due to anti-Christian bias in the U.S. government."

In May 2014, Rev. Franklin Graham said, "Christians are under attack by Islam," when he spoke at the Watchmen on the Wall National Pastors' briefing in Washington, D.C. "The church around the world is under attack. Christians are under attack by Islam. They keep using the word 'radical.' It's not radical; it's just what it is."[64] Islam has an agenda to destroy the church of Jesus Christ, just as it wants to destroy the Jews and Israel. This is why it is so astounding that any church would ever connect itself with Islam.

What would prompt any church to cooperate, unite, or find common ground with Islam? I believe the reason is a centuries' old problem: Divorcing Christianity from her Jewish roots.

Christianity Uprooted

For nearly 2,000 years, the Church has tried to Christianize the Old Testament. In doing this, the Church has became more and more anti-Judaic and anti-Semitic. Ronald Diprose, in his wonderful book, *Israel and the Church: The Origins and Effects of Replacement Theology*, offers this summary of the anti-Semitism which has plagued the church:

> Among the various effects of replacement theology, three must be mentioned at this point. First, the Church tended to establish its own identity in anti-Judaic terms; the Church is what the Jews are no longer or never have been. Second, Christendom's way of interpreting the Old Testament, based on prejudice, has made it very difficult for Jews to take seriously the

---

claim that Jesus of Nazareth is the Messiah of Israel. Third, Christian writers have tended to talk about Israel in the past tense, as may be seen in the convention of terminating histories of Israel with the advent of Christianity or with the fall of the second temple in AD 70.[65]

Replacement theology gets it wrong. God has never stopped seeing His chosen people as a nation. In Jeremiah 31:35-38 (and, similarly, in 33:19-26), God reveals for all to see His perspective regarding the nation of Israel:

Thus says the Lord, who gives the sun for light by day and the fixed order of the moon and the stars for light by night, who stirs up the sea so that its waves roar; the Lord of hosts is His name: "If this fixed order departs from before Me," declares the Lord, "then the offspring of Israel also will cease from being a nation before Me forever."

Here is the test for the Church that these verses provide: If the sun, moon, and stars are still working today, then Israel is still a nation before the Lord. It means the promises, land, covenants, fathers, and law are still theirs, and they have not given up one single thing which God has promised them.

Paul makes this clear in Romans 9:4-5 when he says of his human brothers:

who are Israelites, to whom belongs the adoption as sons and the glory and the covenants and the giving of the Law and the temple service and the promises,

---

65 Ronald E. Diprose, *Israel and the Church: The Origins and Effects of Replacement Theology* (Rome: Institutio Biblico Evangelico Italiano, 2000), 97-98.

whose are the fathers, and from whom is the Christ according to the flesh, who is over all, God blessed forever. Amen.

The problem Israel experiences when she refuses to receive by faith the promises God has given her is the same problem the Church is experiencing. Romans 9:31-32 explains "but Israel, pursuing a law of righteousness, did not arrive at that law. Why? Because they did not pursue it by faith, but as though it were by works. They stumbled over the stumbling stone."

Since Israel does not receive the promises and laws by faith, she misses out on all that God promises. And by denying the promise of God in Jeremiah 31, the Church, too, misses a great joy which is on our Father's heart. God our Father and Jesus, our Jewish Messiah, are still in love with the nation of Israel and her descendants. This care for Israel is clear in Romans 11:28-29:

> From the standpoint of the gospel they [Israel] are enemies for your sake, but from the standpoint of God's choice they are *beloved* for the sake of the fathers; for the gifts and the calling of God are irrevocable. (emphasis mine)

Jeremiah 31 and 33 also affirm that the calling of God is irrevocable. If God still holds the descendants of Abraham, Isaac, and Jacob in high regard as a nation, how can the Church dare to treat them with disdain? God has called the nation of Israel to be a blessing to the world, and He has made it so, but people who are rebellious and disobedient to the Word of God have come to view Israel, the nation, as a supposed evil. God is so clear about this, though, that he reiterates the point strongly in Jeremiah 31:37 where He says: "Thus says the Lord, 'If the heavens above can be measured, and the foundations of the earth searched out below, then I will also cast off all the offspring of Israel for all that they have done,' declares the Lord."

So take notice: God has not cast off His nation which He established by sovereign grace and election based on an unconditional promise! Romans 11 backs up this view when it asks the question in verse 1, "I say then, God has not rejected His people, has He? May it never be!" and in verse 11, "I say then, they did not stumble so as to fall, did they? May it never be!"

This morning, I tested this point to see where we now stand with regard to God's commitment to Israel. When I got up, I checked outside, and the sun came up. My test confirmed that God still has not cast off His nation Israel. This is the same nation which was established again in her land on May 14, 1948. Jeremiah 33:19-21 is a bold confirmation:

> The word of the Lord came to Jeremiah, saying, "Thus says the Lord, 'If you can break My covenant for the day, and My covenant for the night, so that day and night will not be at their appointed time, then My covenant may also be broken with David My servant that he will not have a son to reign on his throne, and with the Levitical priests, My ministers.'"

Israel has survived captivity, and according to Scripture, she will again have a king and priests. God still desires to have Levitical priests before Him because these are unconditional covenants, promises as certain as day and night. You cannot write Israel out of her own Scriptures! God has made that impossible, regardless of what anyone may have done or said to the contrary over the past 2,000 years.

God even rebuked His own people for the evil attitude of rejecting Israel as a nation. Note this dialogue between Jeremiah and the Lord:

> And the word of the Lord came to Jeremiah, saying, "Have you not observed what this people have spoken, saying, 'The two families which the Lord chose, 'He has rejected them'? Thus they despise My people, no longer are they as a nation in their sight. Thus says the Lord, 'If My covenant for the day and night stand not, and the fixed patterns of heaven and earth I have not established, then I would reject the descendants of Jacob and David My servant, not taking from his descendants rulers over the descendants of Abraham, Isaac and Jacob. But I will restore their fortunes and will have mercy on them.'" (Jeremiah 33:23-26)

God reprimanded the Israelites when they claimed they were no longer a nation while captive in Babylon. Those who say God has rejected His two families, Judah and Israel, are opposing God's intended plan to have mercy on His people and restore Israel's fortunes. Numbers 23:19 echoes the immutable nature of the God behind these promises: "God is not a man, that He should lie, nor a son of man, that He should repent; has He said, and will He not do it? Or has He spoken, and will He not make it good?"

In 500 A.D., the Church said Israel is no longer a nation, but God said, "I'm not a man; I don't lie!" In 1000 A.D., Christians claimed Israel is no longer a nation, and God said, "Didn't I call them? I don't change." In 1500, the Church said they are not a nation, and God said, "I spoke, and I will make it good!" In 2016, Catholics, Presbyterians, Methodists, Lutherans, and others are saying Israel is not a nation before the

Lord our God, but God is saying, "YES, THEY ARE!" This rebellion against God's choice of Israel is another reason why the final judgment is on America.

A World at Odds with Israel

During the period just before and after 1948 when God re-established the state of Israel, some critical events took place. Satan is always moving to counteract what God is doing, and in 1917, he saw the British overthrow the Ottoman Empire and capture Jerusalem. At that time, a British politician promised the Jews a home in Palestine, their ancient homeland. This promise was recorded in the Balfour Declaration. Then, as the world moved closer to doing what God prophesied would happen, Satan worked in one of his servants, Adolf Hitler, to try to kill all Jews. As you know, he failed.

In 1947-48, Satan saw what God was doing at the United Nations. On November 24, 1947 when the U.N. voted to re-establish the state of Israel, Satan really needed to kill the Jews, but he bided his time until May 14, 1948. On the day Israel declared herself a new nation, five Arab armies attacked. Since then, movement after movement and nation after nation have tried to destroy Israel, and all have failed, because any such effort is in vain. God, the Shepherd of Israel, will not allow it.

At the same time Israel became a nation, a new organization was formed called the World Council of Churches. The WCC stays on the front lines of attacking the state of Israel. It supports the Boycott Divestment Sanctions (BDS) movement to isolate and punish Jews economically, and it recently supported the Presbyterian Church, USA when the PCUSA divested itself from companies doing business with Israel. On its page for the Palestine Israel Ecumenical Forum, the WCC website, oikoumene.org, says that "WCC urges Christian responsibility in economic measures related to Israeli Palestinian conflict."[66] And what is the "responsibility" it recommends? To divest, boycott, and throw sanctions against Jews so they have no money, no economy, and no nation!

Also in 1948, Satan needed a world movement against the Jews, so he helped establish the Human Rights Commission at the United Nations and its "Universal Declaration of Human Rights." This movement causes the U.N. to censure and attack Israel more than any nation on earth. They are obsessed with demeaning Israel. According to UN Watch (UNWatch. org), in 2013 the U.N. produced 21 resolutions against Israel and only four against all the nations in the rest of the world! Condemning Israel is the preferred pastime of the U.N.

Perhaps it will also seem strange to you that GATT (General Agreement on Trade and Tariffs), WTO (World Trade Organization), and the uniting of banks through computers coincided with followed 1948. The countries are lining up together to attack and destroy this little nation.

Friend in Name Only

We live in significant times, and America can no longer be counted on to support the nation of Israel. While the majority of Americans are pro-Israel, elites in the press, in government, and in our universities are generally anti-Israel. They work tirelessly to undermine the nation of Israel, and more and more, they are finding a willing church and public.

America has already instituted Immorality, Idolatry, and killing Innocents into her laws. Are we about to establish laws against Israel? I fear so. In 2015, the Supreme Court ruled that an American born in Jerusalem cannot claim the baby was

---

66 Oikoumene.org

born in Israel, because in *Zivotosky vs. Kerry, Secretary of State*, the Court had said that the United States had a right *not* to recognize Jerusalem as the capital of Israel. With that decision and the Iranian deal we discussed earlier, the USA is squarely against Israel in law and treaty.

Our nation is dying because we no longer protect our friends or stand up to our enemies. Appeasement of our foes is triggering aggression of all kinds. The pressure points undermining our culture are at an all-time high. In *When Nations Die: America on the Brink*, Jim Nelson Black says we are in the jaws of social, cultural, and moral decay,[67] and he cites a book written by John Lukacs entitled *The End of the Twentieth Century and the End of the Modern Age:*

> For all intents and purposes, Lukacs says, America's power, prestige, and presence in the world are finished. Though its influence may continue for some time, the "American Century" has come to a premature end and America's authority as a source of culture and political convictions is on a rapid downhill slide. What lies ahead, he predicts is a time of troubles that will threaten the very foundation of the modern nation.[68]

Our nation is failing not only because of her sins established in law, she is failing because God wills to remove the power, prestige, and honor which we have held for so long. According to Scripture, all nations eventually come to stand against Israel. This has been declared by God in a variety of scriptures:

- Ezekiel 36:6-7—"Therefore, prophesy concerning the land of Israel, and say to the mountains and

---

67 Black, 1-16.
68 Cited in Black, 259.

to the hills, to the ravines and to the valleys, 'Thus says the Lord God, "Behold, I have spoken in My jealousy and in My wrath because you have endured the insults of the nations." Therefore thus says the Lord God, "I have sworn that surely the nations which are around you will themselves endure their insults."'"

- Ezekiel 37:28—"And the nations will know that I am the Lord who sanctifies Israel, when My sanctuary is in their midst forever."

- Isaiah 34:1-2a—"Draw near, O nations, to hear; and listen, O peoples! Let the earth and all it contains hear, and the world and all that springs from it. For the Lord's indignation is against all the nations, and His wrath against all their armies."

- Zephaniah 3:8—"'Therefore wait for Me,' declares the Lord, 'For the day when I rise up to the prey. Indeed, My decision is to gather nations, to assemble kingdoms, to pour out on them My indignation, all My burning anger; for all the earth will be devoured by the fire of My zeal.'"

We live in a time when the anger of the Lord is burning against the sins of the world. The nations—including America!—are in grave danger. Americans have long had more light and grace from God than any other nation. I only hope we turn and repent so the Lord will be merciful to us in His judgment.

What We Have Learned So Far

1. *Israel, which was scattered by the Lord, has now been gathered by the Lord into the Promised Land.*

2. *God requires all nations to follow His lead in His work with Israel. Yet the nations are failing at this task.*

3. *The Church is divided over Israel into two camps: Those who support this work of God and those who oppose Israel.*

4. *Bad theology produces bad fruit, and good theology produces good fruit.*

5. *America is opposing the work of the Lord with His nation Israel. This is another reason why America is under a final judgment.*

The 'I' Judgments

6

WHAT NOW?

"A son honors his father and a servant his master. Then if I am a father, where is My honor? If I am a master, where is My respect?" says the Lord of Hosts. —Malachi 1:6a

In yet another Old Testament prophecy by Habakkuk, we read of the prophet's disagreement with God over the Divine Plan for Israel. When God tells Habakkuk that He will use Babylon to destroy Judah, the prophet has a serious problem, and in Habakkuk 1:13 the prophet challenges God:

> Your eyes are too pure to approve evil, and You cannot look on wickedness with favor. Why do You look with favor on those who deal treacherously? Why are You silent when the wicked swallow up those more righteous than they?

As bad as Judah had become, Habakkuk argued, are not the Babylonians a lot worse? He pointed out to God that it made no sense for the pure and holy God to use a people far more wicked than Israel to punish Israel.

I feel the same way about America.

As bad as we have become, I still see many great things in America. We still lead the world in giving to charity. When a natural disaster happens, America always shows up to help. Our nation is full of loving, giving people. Our churches are on the forefront of providing for the poor and needy. American churches have provided missionaries and money to bring the gospel to almost every nation on the planet. So why write this book about God judging America when things are still so relatively good here?

Our Last Line of Offense

America has crossed all four lines which the Lord says not to cross. That means: *It does not matter how many good things we are doing—the good does not outweigh the four sins which are pivotal in God's decision to punish and judge a nation.*

Like Habakkuk, I am frustrated and sad that God is bringing judgment to America by those who are more unrighteous than we are, but God is not a respecter of persons—or nations! Crossing the lines that offend God has brought the opportunity of judgment for two overriding reasons:

1. Historically, it is time for God to change the playing field of the nations. He is positioning the nations for the next phase of history.

2. America is being judged on a different standard than most nations have been judged, simply because we have had more light from God than most nations, and "we should know better."

The next phase of history necessitates a new world power. For the last 25 years, America has been the world's lone super power, and I observe that America is tired of leading the world. Intellectual elites are working to undermine our national sovereignty, and the past 20 years have seen pushes for the U.N. to take away our sovereignty. We are even considering instituting a new currency called the Amero, a joint currency between Mexico, Canada, and the U.S. There also have been serious discussions about yielding our sovereignty to the European Union. These conversations among the intellectual elite of the country have become frighteningly serious among politicians—evidence that many have lost hope in America leading the world.

But would it really be so bad if the judgment of God means we lose our sovereignty and have new guards for our security? Wouldn't we be more "united" with the world? Not quite. The truth is, if America gives up her sovereignty, it will be a disaster for many nations. The power of American will, morality, and military has led to peace in Europe and has kept some belligerent nations at bay because of their fear of America. Not surprisingly, those are the nations that desire our downfall and work toward diminishing the power and sovereignty of our great nation.

Wearing US Out

I will tell you more about which nations aspire to our downfall, but first let me tell you something about myself that may not seem relevant, but is. I grew up in the inner city and lived among a people who believed that "might makes right." Gangs tried to bring down anyone who had more power and riches than they did. They were motivated by the crudest form of jealousy, and on the world scene, the United States faces the same low-brow mentality I saw around me in the competition among street gangs.

Since America has long enjoyed more power and riches than any other country, we should expect rivalry and fighting from nations that just don't grasp why we have succeeded the way we have. In 1992, for example, I met a man from Russia who told me that America had "no right" to the power and riches which she had. His reason was simply because we were a historical baby compared to Russia. Another person from China once told me the same thing—America had no right to be "at the top." Two Chinese colonels even wrote a book on how China would destroy America by 2020.[69] It is called *Unrestricted Warfare: China's Master Plan to Destroy America.* Although it was released on August 22, 2002 in America, it had been written three years prior to September 11, 2001. The book outlines how China is attacking America from many directions: economic attacks, computer attacks, attacks on our banks, attacks on our energy infrastructure, even pushing America into wars just to drain our resources. It's all part of a master plan to destroy our country.

What bothers me is that America has not mustered the discernment and strength to call China our enemy. A communist government, driven by atheistic dogma, determined to dominate the world, China has convinced our national leaders that China is our friend. The blindness of our leaders will lead to even greater disaster than we have already experienced.

In a shrewd strategy, China and several other states actively support terror groups that attack America. Our Asian adversary can attack America through "third party" terrorist groups, and we will not say a thing about it. We refuse to connect the dots and continue to simply fight the terrorist groups and not the state sponsors. The war on terror is diminishing the United States, draining our resources, and keeping us from seeing the enemy behind the enemy.

The war on terror is just one example among many that have grown in intensity over the last ten years. Another is America's national debt. Currently over $19,000,000,000,000 (19 trillion dollars), it now surpasses our total gross domestic product—which means we are broke as a nation, living on borrowed time economically—and our moral temperature as a country is not up to the test of another depression. The government is accelerating our debt so radically that at some

---

69 Colonel Qiao Liang and Colonel Wang Xiangsui, *Unrestricted Warfare: China's Master Plan to Destroy America* (Natraj, 2007).

point we will need a bailout, but who will bail us out?

When God judges a nation, He always causes the nation to lose strength for fighting her enemies and lose the desire to protect her money. But there is more.

Another example of God's judgment is drought. According to the *Los Angeles Times*, California is the driest it has been since record keeping began in 1877.

As I prepare this book for publication, the U.S. has signed a "peace" deal with Iran that allows that rogue nation to keep all of her nuclear program intact. It is a very dangerous deal made even more so because, to protect the deal against Congress, the administration has criticized Israel and literally betrayed her to her enemies. We've let other nations down as well. Saudi Arabia and Egypt have let it be known that they have been betrayed by the USA.

We have transgressed the fourth "I," Israel, which we have passed over to our own shame—and great peril. The deal with Iran will bring disfavor from the Lord. Israel sees our rejection so clearly that its Sanhedrin has even put the U.S. president on trial for anti-Semitism and for facilitating the Iranians' destruction of Israel. This is a disaster unlike anything I have seen in my life.

Dangerous Opportunism

Along with Iran, Russia is rising in power. It has taken over the Crimea, attacked the Ukraine, and become an ally to Iran. The Iranian deal further empowers the Russians against the USA. One general went so far as to threaten nuclear war with America, and another claimed Russia would attack Europe if the Americans moved into the Baltic states. So far, America has moved troops into the Baltic states, and Russia has responded by moving troops into the Ukraine. Russian military jets have made threatening forays into our airspace without an appropriate American response.

To heighten the threat, Russia owns a weapon called the Club K car, a container that can be put on trains and transport ships. While the container looks like any other standard international shipping container, it contains missile launchers. The system is designed so that Russia (or one of its allies) could place a Club K car on a ship entering New York Harbor, for instance, and launch a nuclear missile into the atmosphere. Exploding the warhead above the earth's surface would create what is called an Electromagnetic Pulse (EMP). The energy wave would knock out the electrical system across the nation. A Congressional report on the magnitude of disaster that would result said we could be set back to the 1800s with no cell phones, electricity, or electronic devices whatsoever. Most vehicles would cease to function as well.

The Russians are militarily aggressive, and the U.S. Secretary of Defense has called the Russians an existential threat to America. Russia is a major danger to our national safety. The country has nukes and ways to deliver them to America that other nations do not have. Yet as Vladimir Putin continues to threaten the United States, America does not respond.

Three top U.S. military leaders have publicly acknowledged that Russia has the capability to wipe America off the map because of the hoard of nuclear weapons Russia has stockpiled. Admiral Gordon, for instance, testified to Congress that Russia was deploying intercontinental ballistic missiles aimed at the USA, and TU Bear bombers that carry 12 cruise missiles armed with nukes have been flying at both our Pacific and Atlantic coasts. The Russian SS-300 and SS-400 missile system is better than ours, and these surface to air missiles are being deployed along with the new SS-500 system. The Obama administration, though, has made it equally public that it does not agree with the assessment of our own generals.

Adding the aggressive nature of Russian behavior to its client state of Iran can spell disaster for America. Just as the prophet Habakkuk complained about the Lord using Babylon to destroy Judah, we could claim that America is more righteous than Russia and Iran. And we might be right—but that doesn't change our accountability before God.

In the last few years, America has failed to look after her friends. We refused to put up a missile defense system for Poland and Eastern Europe. Every time America moved toward protecting the Europeans, Russia raised objections, and we backed off. The breaking of our promises to Ukraine, Poland, and the Baltic states seems to extend to the USA itself. We refuse even to prepare a defense against the Russian nuclear threat aimed at us. We now have fewer than 2,000 warheads which, according to experts, makes America vulnerable to a nuclear first strike by Russia; some say we have only 1,500 warheads. This is an especially serious problem because Russia has a better defense than we do against nuclear attack. The Russians now believe, in fact, that they can survive a first strike against America. Nevertheless, the Obama administration is deaf to the warnings of our generals.

Will God use Russia against America, or will He use several nations at the same time? The world scene has created many who would no doubt like to be chosen for the job.

Down Time

God raises up nations and brings them down, and the evidence coming in these days is that God is bringing down America. He expects nations to repent when He speaks to them—especially those who have His light. Since America has not repented, though, we have laid ourselves open to the reality that God can do with America whatever He desires, like clay in a potter's hand.

America is in the hands of the Lord, and the judgment on America will not be like the judgment on the nations of Amos 1 and 2. We have a Christian heritage and know the truth; therefore *we should know better.* We should know not to kill innocent babies in the womb; we should know not to support gay marriage, adultery, and pre-marital sex. We should know not to throw God out of the culture, schools, courthouses, and public square. We should know not to support those who wish to destroy Israel.

I lament greatly that the nations and churches of the world have not helped Israel in the return to her land. God promised to bring back the twelve tribes of Israel and is doing it. Yet the nations once again are rebelling at what God is doing in history, and even though America is in a unique position to help Israel, we have fallen far short in the opportunity.

There is no need to compare ourselves to other nations. Despite all of the money and protection we have provided Israel, we have now betrayed her. We have made treaties with her deadliest enemies, with those who want nothing more than her complete annihilation.

And why have we not declared Jerusalem the capital of Israel? Why have we pushed a two-state solution to the Palestinian issue? Why have we demanded that Israel give up territory? Dividing the land of Israel brings the wrath of God!

I wish I could assure you of personal "good times" in the coming judgment, but the hard truth is that, when a nation is being judged by God, the righteous suffer along with the unrighteous. The examples in Scripture are numerous. Daniel was carried into captivity along with everyone else because of the sins of his nation, and he served in the court of the heathen king Nebuchadnezzar. Ezekiel was a captive with his people in order to be a witness to his countrymen. Joshua and Caleb had to march around the wilderness for 40 years with their faithless brother and sister Israelites. Yet they served Israel faithfully by leading its armies.

As God is bringing judgment on America, remember that you have a role to play. Our attitude should be that of Habakkuk:

> Though the fig tree should not blossom, and there be no fruit on the vines, though the yield of the olive should fail and the fields produce no food, though the flock should be cut off from the fold and there be no cattle in the stalls, yet I will exalt in the LORD, I will rejoice in the God of my salvation. The Lord God is my strength, and He makes my feet like hinds feet, and makes me walk on my high places. (Habbakuk 3:17-19)

During times of judgment, you will have opportunity to testify to the Lord's greatness, so be faithful and persevere to the end.

And lest you despair, let me assure you that there is great hope. The gospel—the good news of God's work through Jesus Christ—can *and will* change hearts and minds. God can bring revival to the nation through His gospel. Its good news tells how sin, which brings the judgment of God, can be paid for by the blood of Jesus Christ.

The gospel is built upon the truth of a substitutionary atonement as described in Romans 5:8: "But God demonstrates His own love toward us, in that while we were yet sinners, Christ died for us." The gospel is a demonstration of love by God. He poured His wrath on Himself in the person of His Son Jesus Christ. Jesus, who is fully man and fully God, took the whole weight of God's wrath so we do not have to.

Jesus' death is a victory because He rose from the dead

three days later and is alive today. He is working in the nations through His people and working through His children in America to bring people to their senses and deny Immorality, Idolatry, killing Innocents, and racism in all its forms.

Anyone who bows and serves Jesus as King of Kings and Lord of Lords will find purpose in life, no matter what happens to the nation in which he or she happens to live. As Ephesians 2:8-9 says, "For by grace you have been saved through faith; and that not of yourselves, it is the gift of God, not a result of works, that no one should boast."

If you put your faith in Jesus and trust in Him, then you must believe in your heart that God raised Jesus from the dead, that He is the King, that He is coming again, and confess Him before others. Jesus is worthy of this because He is the Messiah, the Holy One of Israel who has been exalted to the right hand of God. He is the One who holds the nations of the world in His hands.

My prayer for you is that you trust God in everything that comes and experience His joy and peace. And that by His grace, you persevere!